OXFORD WORLD'S CLASSICS

REVERIES OF THE
SOLITARY WALKER

JEAN-JACQUES ROUSSEAU (1712–78) was born in Geneva, at that time an independent republic of which Rousseau would proudly call himself a citizen. His mother, Suzanne Bernard, died soon after his birth. His father, Isaac Rousseau, a watchmaker, left Geneva when his son was 10, leaving him in the care of relatives. In 1728 Rousseau decided to seek his fortune elsewhere. He served as a domestic in a prominent Turin family, but he found a new home in Chambéry with Mme de Warens, who acted by turns as his mother, mentor, and lover. He taught himself philosophy and literature, worked briefly as a tutor in Lyons, and in 1742 arrived in Paris, where he met Diderot and Condillac, as well as Thérèse Levasseur, his lifelong companion. After the success of his *Discourse on the Sciences and the Arts* (1750), which criticized the corrupting influence of civilization, he resigned his position as secretary in the wealthy Dupin family and from then on supported himself by his pen, although he continued to enjoy the hospitality of enlightened aristocrats. He wrote articles on music and political economy for Diderot's *Encyclopaedia*, and an opera, *The Village Soothsayer*. The *Discourse on Inequality* appeared in 1755, and a polemical *Letter to d'Alembert on Theatre* in 1758.

Rousseau's novel, *Julie, or the New Héloïse* (1761), was greeted enthusiastically, but *The Social Contract*, his boldest political work, and his treatise on education, *Émile* (both 1762), were condemned as subversive. Fleeing arrest, Rousseau travelled in Switzerland, where he began his autobiographical *Confessions* (published posthumously), to England at the invitation of David Hume, and back to the French provinces, where, his mind increasingly troubled, he lived under a pseudonym. He was allowed to return to Paris in 1770, where he composed his *Reveries of the Solitary Walker*. He died at Ermenonville outside Paris in 1778.

RUSSELL GOULBOURNE is Professor of Early Modern French Literature at the University of Leeds. He has published widely on seventeenth- and eighteenth-century French literature and has contributed to the new critical edition of Voltaire's complete works. He has translated Diderot's *The Nun* for Oxford World's Classics.

OXFORD WORLD'S CLASSICS

For over 100 years Oxford World's Classics have brought readers closer to the world's great literature. Now with over 700 titles—from the 4,000-year-old myths of Mesopotamia to the twentieth century's greatest novels—the series makes available lesser-known as well as celebrated writing.

The pocket-sized hardbacks of the early years contained introductions by Virginia Woolf, T. S. Eliot, Graham Greene, and other literary figures which enriched the experience of reading. Today the series is recognized for its fine scholarship and reliability in texts that span world literature, drama and poetry, religion, philosophy and politics. Each edition includes perceptive commentary and essential background information to meet the changing needs of readers.

OXFORD WORLD'S CLASSICS

JEAN-JACQUES ROUSSEAU

Reveries of the Solitary Walker

Translated with an Introduction and Notes by
RUSSELL GOULBOURNE

OXFORD
UNIVERSITY PRESS

OXFORD

UNIVERSITY PRESS

Great Clarendon Street, Oxford OX2 6DP

Oxford University Press is a department of the University of Oxford.
It furthers the University's objective of excellence in research, scholarship,
and education by publishing worldwide in

Oxford New York

Auckland Cape Town Dar es Salaam Hong Kong Karachi
Kuala Lumpur Madrid Melbourne Mexico City Nairobi
New Delhi Shanghai Taipei Toronto

With offices in

Argentina Austria Brazil Chile Czech Republic France Greece
Guatemala Hungary Italy Japan Poland Portugal Singapore
South Korea Switzerland Thailand Turkey Ukraine Vietnam

Oxford is a registered trade mark of Oxford University Press
in the UK and in certain other countries

Published in the United States
by Oxford University Press Inc., New York

British Library Cataloguing in Publication Data

Data available

Library of Congress Cataloging in Publication Data

Data available

Typeset by Glyph International, Bangalore, India
Printed in Great Britain
on acid-free paper by
Clays Ltd, St Ives plc

ISBN 978-0-19-956327-2

1 3 5 7 9 10 8 6 4 2

ACKNOWLEDGEMENTS

I AM grateful to the many colleagues and friends who have generously given me their help and advice, in particular David Coward, Alison Fell, Richard Hibbitt, Catherine Kaiserman, David McCallam, Nigel Saint, and Edward Welch. I should also like to thank Judith Luna for being an unfailingly patient and supportive editor. My greatest debt, though, is to Lisa Needham, who, in our rural retreat, has shown me that it really is better not to be a solitary walker after all: to her this volume is gratefully dedicated.

CONTENTS

INTRODUCTION

AT the beginning of his poem 'Sylvie's Walk' ('L'Allée de Sylvie', 1747), written nearly thirty years before he began the *Reveries of the Solitary Walker* (*Les Rêveries du promeneur solitaire*), Jean-Jacques Rousseau strikes a note that seems to resonate throughout his career:

> As I wander freely in these groves,
> My heart the highest pleasure knows!
> How happy I am under the shady trees!
> How I love the silvery streams!
> Sweet and charming reverie,
> Dear and beloved solitude,
> May you always be my true delight!

Inspired by a walk beside the river Cher at Chenonceaux, where Rousseau was living with the Dupin family, for whom he worked as a secretary, the poem evokes the ecstasies of wandering, nature, solitude, and reverie—all of which anticipate the poetic prose of the *Reveries*. However, the poem has none of the later text's invasive sense of anxiety, hostility, persecution, and torment. For as much as Rousseau's early poem and his last work seem to have in common, the Rousseau who wrote the *Reveries* was very different from the Rousseau who wrote 'Sylvie's Walk': if the poem is the work of a self-taught musician-cum-writer, increasingly well-connected, if not terribly well known, making his way working for wealthy patrons and writing, amongst other things, articles on music to be published in Diderot and d'Alembert's freethinking *Encyclopaedia* (*L'Encyclopédie*, 1751–72), the *Reveries*, by contrast, come from the pen of an international celebrity, a writer who had achieved overnight fame—and infamy—with an eloquent denunciation of the corrupting influence of celebrity-obsessed society.

Everything changed for Rousseau with the publication in early 1751, when he was thirty-eight, of his first book, the *Discourse on the*

Sciences and the Arts (*Discours sur les sciences et les arts*). Written in
response to an essay competition set the previous year by the Dijon
Academy, the text argues, paradoxically, that intellectual progress
has fostered moral corruption and a decline in civic virtue. Here
Rousseau launches upon a theme that will, in a variety of different
guises, preoccupy him for the rest of his life: put simply, the relationship between self and other. From the 1750s onwards he will
be centrally concerned with the problems of man in society and
with the tensions between society and nature. These problems
and tensions he explores in works as diverse as the *Discourse on
Inequality* (*Discours sur l'origine et les fondements de l'inégalité*,
1755), in which he argues that inequalities of rank, wealth, and
power are the inevitable result of the civilizing process; the *Letter
to d'Alembert on Theatre* (*Lettre à d'Alembert sur les spectacles*,
1758), in which he argues that theatre is morally dangerous because
it encourages audiences to cut themselves off from public society
and indulge the most suspect of emotions; *Julie, or the New Héloïse*
(*Julie ou la Nouvelle Héloïse*, 1761), one of the century's best-
selling novels, a patriarchal idyll about the importance of transfer-
ring erotic longing into virtuous restraint; *Émile, or On Education*
(*Émile ou De l'éducation*, 1762), a treatise on education which
opens with a clear statement of Rousseau's core vision of human
agency's corrupting influence: 'All is good when it leaves the hands
of the Author of all things, all degenerates in the hands of man';
and *The Social Contract* (*Du Contrat social*, 1762), Rousseau's
major work of political philosophy, in which he sets out his vision
for a just and humane political community. With these works he
adds powerful new brushstrokes to his sombre portrait of what has
happened to humankind as a result of so-called progress and civilization, dissecting the forces at work that conspire to alienate
humankind from their true nature. Rousseau, who proudly
attached his name to all of these works (in contrast to his contemporary Voltaire, for instance, who had recourse to innumerable
pseudonyms, as well as to anonymity, when publishing his controversial texts), was not afraid to take on dearly held Enlightenment
convictions—such as the belief in progress—and show them to be
mere assumptions and unproven contentions.

Moreover, it is precisely Rousseau's well-publicized and polemical views on society which brought him not only the celebrity he loathed but also the infamy that saw him, in his terms, driven into exile, unfairly rejected by his fellow men. In this respect, 1762 is a turning-point. Having left Paris and its literary scene in 1756, and having severed ties first with his patron Mme d'Épinay, the hostess of a famous salon, at the end of 1757 and subsequently with his sometime friends Diderot and Friedrich Melchior Grimm, an intimate of Mme d'Épinay's, in 1762 Rousseau was plunged into controversy by the publication of *Émile*, which, primarily because of the religious views Rousseau expressed in it, was condemned by the Paris *parlement*, who also issued an arrest warrant for its author. Rousseau now became convinced that there was a conspiracy against him, and this sense of persecution was to remain with him for the rest of his life. He renounced his citizenship of his native Geneva, whose authorities had also condemned him and his works, and the rest of the 1760s he spent in a kind of exile, leaving France for Switzerland, including his brief but idyllic stay on the Île de St Pierre in the Lac de Bienne, followed by an ill-fated journey to England in 1766, made at the invitation of the Scottish philosopher and historian David Hume, with whom Rousseau ended up quarrelling. He returned to France in 1767 and lived in the provinces, only returning to Paris in 1770.

In response to the events of 1762 and their traumatic repercussions, Rousseau's gaze turned inward and he wrote, if not a trilogy in the strict sense of the term, then a kind of triptych of autobiographical works. The first of these, the *Confessions*, which Rousseau started writing in 1764, are addressed to his contemporaries as he seeks to reshape the perception of his work and correct the misrepresentations of him. Determined to exonerate himself, Rousseau seeks to set out logically and systematically what he calls in Book 7 of the work the 'chain of feelings' that marked the successive stages of his being.[1] Between November 1770 and

---

[1] J.-J. Rousseau, *Confessions*, trans. Angela Scholar, ed. Patrick Coleman (Oxford: Oxford University Press, 2000), 270. All subsequent references will be included in the text.

May 1771 he gave readings from his work to aristocrats in Paris, though these so embarrassed Mme d'Épinay that she petitioned the police to ban them. The reaction he received to his reading at the home of the comtesse d'Egmont in 1771 was so remarkable that he ends the *Confessions* with it: 'No one spoke' (p. 642), he tells us on the last page.

Beset by paranoia, Rousseau's next step, it seems, was to divide himself in two and write, between 1772 and 1776, the three dialogues that make up *Rousseau Judge of Jean-Jacques: Dialogues* (*Rousseau juge de Jean-Jacques: Dialogues*), in which 'Rousseau' and 'a Frenchman' discuss the life and works of Jean-Jacques (Rousseau himself). The role played by the Frenchman in the text is crucial: so dismayed was he by his failure to win over the putative readers of his *Confessions* that Rousseau, through the Frenchman, effectively incorporates the reader in the *Dialogues* and has his alter ego, 'Rousseau', set about persuading him. The *Dialogues* also envisage the judgement of posterity, and, gripped by mental torment, Rousseau tried to place the manuscript of the *Dialogues* on the High Altar of the cathedral of Notre-Dame, Paris, on 24 February 1776 but found his way was barred by a gate. His sense of alienation and persecution was all but complete.

Having first been ignored and then divided himself in two, Rousseau finally turns in on himself in his *Reveries*, his last attempt to achieve some kind of mental and spiritual balance in his life. The turning-point seems to come with the death on 2 August 1776 of the prince de Conti, his sometime protector (and great-grandson of the prince de Conti who had protected Molière), if indeed this is what he is alluding to when he states in the First Walk that 'an event as sad as it was unforeseen' has shown him that his 'earthly fate is irrevocably fixed for evermore' (p. 5): with the prince de Conti's death, it seems, dies Rousseau's last hope of being rehabilitated. Whatever the event, it clearly triggered a change of mood and inspired Rousseau to write the *Reveries*, on which he worked from September 1776 to April 1778, leaving them unfinished at his death three months later; they were first published, like the *Confessions*, in 1782.

The *Reveries* are a kind of continuation of, or appendix to, but not actually the planned third part of, the *Confessions*.[2] It is true that they tell us some things about Rousseau's life that the *Confessions* did not, such as the episodes with his cousin Fazy and his friend Pleince recounted in the Fourth Walk. But crucially the two works are different in character and scope. Whereas in the *Confessions* Rousseau seeks to explain himself to others, in the *Reveries*, by contrast, he makes a point of addressing only himself, since all he seeks, as he spells out in the First Walk, is to understand himself: 'But what about me, cut off from them and from everything else, what am I? . . . I am devoting my last days to studying myself' (pp. 3, 7). In the *Reveries* Rousseau eschews chronology and a narrative stressing cause and effect in favour of reflection, self-analysis, and meditation. His narrative is resolutely non-linear and profoundly introspective and personal, 'the desire to be better known by people', as he also remarks in the First Walk, having 'died in [his] heart' (p. 9).

Whereas the *Confessions* enact a kind of moral vivisection—*Intus, et in cute* ('underneath, and in the flesh'), as the epigraph from Persius puts it (p. 5)—the *Reveries*, by contrast, show Rousseau apparently accepting himself and endeavouring to give himself the space in which to express himself and feel as never before what it means to exist. This is, in principle at least, neither a confessional nor a polemical work; rather, it is a work in which, as he remarks in the First Walk, he gives himself over entirely to 'the pleasure of conversing with [his] soul, for this is the only pleasure that [his] fellow men cannot take away from [him]' (p. 7). And therein, for Rousseau, lies the crux of the text: it is intended as a poignant response to, and an extended rebellion against, those who have tried to control him. Rousseau says that he finds strength in indifference towards his enemies and persecutors, and happiness in solitude amidst nature. Long reflection on his plight as a victim of persecution leads Rousseau to conclude from the outset—hence

---

[2] At the end of the twelfth and final book of the *Confessions*, which is divided into two parts, Rousseau refers to a putative third part, which will only appear 'if ever I summon up the strength to write it' (p. 642). Similarly, in Books 7 and 8 he refers to the need to write a supplement to the work (pp. 316, 373).

the all-important 'so' in the very first sentence of the *Reveries*, suggesting a summing up of, and a conclusion to, previous reflection—that he must accept his fate, stop fighting against it, and be, as he claims in the First Walk, 'at peace in the depths of the chasm, a poor, unfortunate mortal, but as impassive as God himself' (p. 7). He appears to move from his earlier modes of confession, self-defence, and self-justification to a stoic, self-sufficient acceptance of his fate and thereby an apparent triumph over those who seek to control him: his introspection leads him to seek out and find a remedy for his sufferings in those sufferings themselves. In other words, he turns isolation and solitude to his own advantage. He revels in the fact that, in spite of themselves, his enemies have given him an opportunity he gladly embraces: the opportunity to be alone. As he says in the Seventh Walk: 'This is my way of taking revenge on my persecutors: I can think of no crueller way of punishing them than to be happy in spite of them' (p. 70).

But is the Rousseau of the *Reveries* as happy as he claims to be? Has he really avenged himself of those whom he believes to be his persecutors? The text in fact gives no unambiguous answers to such questions. On the contrary, it gives voice to contradictions and obsessions which give us a very sharp sense of a Rousseau still working through the problems he claims to have overcome. Most obviously, this is a text shot through with such a vivid sense of there being widespread hostility towards Rousseau that it is difficult to accept that he is merely indifferent to misfortune and persecution. In addition, thoroughgoing self-analysis does not prevent Rousseau from engaging in more or less subtle self-defence, even self-exoneration: whereas, from the outset, his persecutors are characterized by their extravagant cruelty ('in the refinement of their hatred they have continued to seek out the cruellest forms of torture for my sensitive soul', p. 3), he praises himself, in contrast, as 'the most sociable and loving of human beings' (p. 3) and, later, as 'the most trusting of men' (p. 64) and 'the most sensitive of beings' (p. 84); in the Fourth Walk, Rousseau deftly embeds his passing, even self-pitying admission that he lied as a youth about the theft of a ribbon, and had a kitchen maid sacked to save himself, within a complex argument about the relativity of truth and falsehood, an argument that ultimately celebrates the man—implicitly Rousseau himself—who holds to truth to the point of self-sacrifice; and in the Ninth Walk, his oblique attempt to rationalize his decision to place in the Foundlings' Hospital the five children he had between 1746 and 1751 with his long-time companion Thérèse Levasseur is set within an elaborate, self-justificatory illustration of how good he is with children. And lastly, whatever we may think of Rousseau's view of himself and of others, it is difficult not to be moved by the suggestions in his text that he is not as happy as he claims to be: for instance, having noted at the end of the Seventh Walk, with now familiar but nevertheless striking recourse to hyperbole, that he is still 'in the midst of the most miserable fate ever endured by a mortal' (p. 82), in the Ninth Walk he goes on to give pained expression to his insatiable longing for happiness with other human beings:

Oh, if I could still enjoy a few moments of pure, heartfelt affection, even if only from a babe in arms, if I could still see in people's eyes the joy and satisfaction of being with me, how these brief but sweet effusions of my heart would compensate me for so many woes and afflictions. Ah, I would no longer be obliged to seek among animals the kind looks that I am now refused by human beings. (pp. 97–8)

There is here none of the God-like impassivity and self-sufficiency he claims for himself elsewhere in the text (pp. 7, 19, 55–6); on the contrary, this is the very human Rousseau who lays himself bare, in all his weakness and fallibility, through the words on the page.

It follows, then, that this is no straightforward text about a man fleeing society and finding happiness in total seclusion. It is true that as early as 1756, as Rousseau records in Book 9 of his *Confessions*, the great critic of society felt the need to be on his own: 'There I was at last, then, at home in my own pleasant and secluded retreat, master of my days, free to spend them living that independent, even, and peaceful life for which I felt I had been born' (p. 403). But Rousseau's love of solitude is not simply a form of misanthropy, since he also insists from the outset on his own sociability. What he turns away from is not society per se, but rather the forms of social contact and interaction that supposedly polite society expects of him, notably conversation, an art at which he feels he does not excel, as he makes clear in the Fourth Walk (p. 42). What he is opposed to is what he sees as the opacity that contemporary social relations impose between people. Solitude is a response to the specific realities of a particular society, since that society cannot in principle provide the kind of interaction he desires: the strictly codified norms of courteous behaviour are repellent for Rousseau, since they impede, according to him, true communication and undermine authentic sociability. It is precisely because his desire for authentic sociability is frustrated by conventional society that Rousseau feels alienated from it, and this is why he escapes the world of men in order to recover the true nature of things.

From the demands of corrupt society Rousseau turns to the world of nature. Walking alone in nature guarantees and even intensifies his sense of self, as he observes in the Second Walk: 'These hours of solitude and meditation are the only time of the day when I am completely myself, without distraction or hindrance, and when I can truly say that I am what nature intended me to be' (p. 11). His happiness comes in part from his being at one with nature, which was a refuge for Rousseau from the anxieties of life, providing him with relative solitude and a rich source of distractions, both of which offer him peace of mind: the Île de St Pierre, described with such memorable intensity and poetic vividness in the Fifth Walk, is a kind of asylum, a prison where Rousseau would gladly be holed up for the rest of his days, the island's isolation mirroring his own desire to live a carefully circumscribed life. Rousseau finds hope in the refuge of nature, and in so doing he offered future generations of people living with anxiety the possibility of an inspired cure.

The diversity of nature keeps Rousseau busy and helps him not to think unpleasant, unwanted thoughts. Rousseau delves into this diversity through his interest in botany. If, in the Seventh Walk, Rousseau presents botany as an easy, even lazy pastime, this cannot hide the fact that he was, in reality, a serious, even systematic botanist, as suggested not only by the Fifth Walk, but also by his surviving herbaria, his correspondence with leading French botanists such as Pierre Clappier and Marc-Antoine Claret de La Tourrette, and such posthumously published works as the *Elementary Letters on Botany* (*Lettres élémentaires sur la botanique*), which he wrote to teach botany to Madeleine-Catherine Delessert, the daughter of his long-standing friend Mme Boy de la Tour, and the *Fragments for a Dictionary of Botanical Terms* (*Fragments pour un dictionnaire des termes d'usage en botanique*), both of which he worked on in the early 1770s. It is unsurprising, then, that Rousseau should posit a kind of parallel between his work as a botanist and his aims in writing the *Reveries*, for he is to be as scientific in one as he is in the other, hence the image in the First Walk of the 'barometer' and the soul as a kind of natural element to be measured (p. 9). He is the writer-scientist whose object of analysis is himself.

This self-analysis is structured around a series of ten walks, the last left unfinished at Rousseau's death. Walking was Rousseau's preferred mode of transport. From an early age he developed what he calls in Book 2 of the *Confessions* a 'passion for walking' (p. 53), and the journeys he seems to prefer are those guided by chance: he delights in peripatetic randomness, or what he calls 'the pleasures of going one knows not where' (p. 57). Such walks, crucially, allow his mind to wander, too, as he tellingly observes in Book 9: 'I can meditate only when walking; as soon as I stop, I can no longer think, for my mind moves only when my feet do' (p. 400). To walk is to meditate and to muse. In the midst of nature, Rousseau finds freedom to think, as he explains in Book 4:

There is something about walking that animates and activates my ideas; I can hardly think at all when I am still; my body must move if my mind is to do the same. The pleasant sights of the countryside, the unfolding scene, the good air, a good appetite, the sense of well-being that returns as I walk . . . all of this releases my soul, encourages more daring flights of thought, impels me, as it were, into the immensity of being, which I can choose from, appropriate, and combine exactly as I wish. (p. 158)

These 'flights of thought' are the essence of the reveries that give Rousseau's last work its title.

Rousseau was not the first to write about reverie. We know from Book 1 of the *Confessions* (pp. 8–9) that Rousseau was from an early age an avid reader of romance fiction, including the works of Madeleine de Scudéry, who, in Part 2 of her *Clélie* (1654–60), shows Cléodamas and Bérélise in a garden, giving themselves over to the charms of reverie, a state of heightened sensibility and inner pleasure, freed from social constraints. For these characters, reverie is a passing moment of release and interiority. A similar sense of release is conveyed, albeit in a very different form, in Bernard le Bovier de Fontenelle's *Conversations on the Plurality of Worlds* (*Entretiens sur la pluralité des mondes*, 1686), which also figured amongst Rousseau's early reading: the philosopher conversing with a Marquise in her garden at night gazes up at the stars and is plunged into a reverie, a delightful 'disorder of thoughts'. This notion of the lessening of the power of reason and the emphasis on feeling also appeal to the sensualist philosophers of the eighteenth century, amongst them Étienne Bonnot de Condillac, who evokes the freedom of reverie in his *Essay on the Origin of Human Knowledge* (*Essai sur l'origine des connaissances humaines*, 1746): after a hard day's work, he argues, the mind enjoys seeing ideas 'floating around haphazardly', particularly when this 'disorder' is matched by the freedom of nature as opposed to the manicured order of landscaped gardens. Momentarily removed from the world and its preoccupations, the one who gives himself over to reverie finds the pleasure of freedom in nature.

But whereas all these earlier writers envisage reverie as a kind of momentary escape, for Rousseau, by contrast, reverie is a way of life, an ongoing means of triumphing over the grim realities of the existence that others seek to impose on him. He makes of it, not a passing phase, but a key to his existence, and crucially a key to his overcoming his enemies: meditation and (self-)mastery are as one. And more than that, for Rousseau reverie is also a means of storing up a treasure trove of happy memories that will in turn bring him happiness in the future. Reverie revives the past and ensures its survival; writing, reading, and rereading are all integral to Rousseau's pursuit of happiness, as he explains in the First Walk:

The leisure of my daily walks has often been filled with delightful thoughts which I am sorry to have forgotten. I shall preserve in writing those which come to me in the future: every time I reread them I shall experience the pleasure of them again. . . . If, as I hope, I have the same cast of mind when I am very old and as the moment of my departure approaches, reading them will remind me of the pleasure I have in writing them and, by thus reviving the past for me, will double my existence, so to speak. In spite of men I shall still be able to enjoy the delights of company, and, grown decrepit, I shall live with myself in another age, as if living with a younger friend. (pp. 8–9)

The memory of past happiness creates pleasure for him in the present of writing and will, in turn, create pleasure for him in a later present as a reader. Reverie is part and parcel of a search for lasting happiness: Rousseau's vision of happiness takes root in, and is a means of coming to terms with, the realities of unhappiness and anxiety. Reverie is also an epistemological project: writing down his thoughts is a way of his establishing the truth about himself. Whereas in the *Confessions* Rousseau was concerned with historical fact, in the *Reveries* he is concerned with the sensations of the past and happiness in the future. Writing becomes for Rousseau a means of recovering lost time: it is, in that sense, its own cure.

The idea that the *Reveries* are a kind of remedy for Rousseau finds an echo in the way in which, in the First Walk, he positions his text vis-à-vis Michel de Montaigne's *Essays* (*Essais*, 1580–95). Having, in Book 10 of the *Confessions*, poured scorn on what he saw as 'the false naivety of Montaigne, who, while pretending to confess his faults, is very careful to give himself only lovable ones' (p. 505), at the beginning of the *Reveries*, Rousseau at once likens his project to, and distances it from, that of his sixteenth-century predecessor: 'My task is the same as that of Montaigne, but my aim is the exact opposite of his: for he wrote his essays entirely for others, whereas I am writing my reveries entirely for myself' (p. 9). Of course, Montaigne's *Essays* were not quite so public as Rousseau wishes to present them: in his prefatory address 'To the Reader' ('Au Lecteur'), Montaigne stresses that he has set himself 'no other end but a private family one', adding: 'I have dedicated this book to the private benefit of my friends and kinsmen so that, having lost me (as they must do soon), they can find here again xx *Introduction*

some traits of my characters and of my humours.'[3] This notwith-standing, the numerous links between Montaigne's *Essays* and Rousseau's *Reveries* are important and add further levels of meaning to the later text.

First, both texts offer self-portraits of thinking, reflective, medi-tative men. In his chapter 'On Practice' ('De l'exercitation', II. 6), for example, Montaigne identifies an organic link between think-ing and being that will lie at the heart of Rousseau's text: 'I am chiefly portraying my ways of thinking, a shapeless subject which simply does not become manifest in deeds. . . . It is not what I do that I write of, but of me, of what I *am*.'[4] Secondly, both texts take the form of reveries. On several occasions Montaigne uses the French term 'rêverie' to describe his own writing, though he delib-erately plays with the negative connotations of the term (which persisted in eighteenth-century dictionary definitions, too). For example, he begins his chapter 'On Educating Children' ('De l'institution des enfants', I. 26) with the witty disclaimer: 'These writings of mine are no more than the ravings [*rêveries*] of a man who has never done more than taste the outer crust of knowledge.'[5] He goes further still in his chapter 'On Books' ('Des livres', II. 10):

These are my own thoughts, by which I am striving to make known not matter but me. . . . I have no sergeant-major to marshal my arguments other than Fortune. As my ravings [*rêveries*] present themselves, I pile them up; sometimes they all come crowding together, sometimes they drag along in single file. I want people to see my natural ordinary stride, however much it wanders off the path. I let myself go along as I find myself to be.[6]

For Montaigne, 'rêverie' is a self-mocking term used with ironic modesty both to justify the fragmentary nature of his work and to invite a playful reading of it. Montaigne appears to be saying that it is sheer madness to write what he does and, worse still, to offer oneself as the subject.

Montaigne's playfulness here, evoking the movement of his thoughts and his own wanderings, points to a third link between

[3] Michel de Montaigne, *The Complete Essays*, trans. and ed. M. A. Screech (London: Allen Lane, 1991), p. lix.

[4] Ibid. 425–6.   [5] Ibid. 163.   [6] Ibid. 457, 459.

his *Essays* and Rousseau's *Reveries*: they are both texts written 'on the go'. In his chapter 'On Three Kinds of Social Intercourse' ('De trois commerces', III. 3), he describes how, in his library, 'sometimes my mind wanders off, at others I walk to and fro, noting down and dictating these whims of mine';[7] and in his chapter 'On Some Lines of Virgil' ('Sur des vers de Virgile', III. 5), Montaigne describes how sometimes he thinks best while he is on the move:

But what displeases me about my soul is that she usually gives birth quite unexpectedly, when I am least on the lookout for them, to her profoundest, her maddest ravings [*rêveries*] which please me most. Then they quickly vanish away because, then and there, I have nothing to jot them down on; it happens when I am on my horse or at table or in bed—especially on my horse, the seat of my widest musings.[8]

For Rousseau, too, musings and movement go hand in hand. Walking is, as he notes in Book 3 of the *Confessions*, thought-inspiring: 'Seated at my table, with my pen in my hand and my paper in front of me, I have never been able to achieve anything. It is when I am out walking among the rocks and the woods, it is at night, sleepless in my bed, that I write in my head' (p. 111). This link between musings and movement, mentioned incidentally in the *Essays* and the *Confessions*, is fundamental to the *Reveries*, both etymologically—the French term *rêverie* is derived from the Latin verb *vagari*, meaning to wander or to roam about—and even literally, since Rousseau based his text on notes he had scribbled down on twenty-seven playing cards while out walking, which were found amongst his papers after his death.[9]

Perhaps the last and potentially most far-reaching thing that Montaigne's *Essays* and Rousseau's *Reveries* have in common is that both texts attempt to portray the twists and turns of each writer's mind. Like Montaigne before him, Rousseau forges his identity through a process of spontaneous mental combustion,

[7] Ibid. 933.

[8] Ibid. 990–1.

[9] These playing cards, which are now in the Bibliothèque publique et universitaire in Neuchâtel, are helpfully reproduced in J.-J. Rousseau, *Les Rêveries du promeneur solitaire*, ed. F. S. Eigeldinger (Paris: Honoré Champion, 2010), 171–225.

through the accumulation of thoughts and memories: like the *Essays*, the *Reveries* paint the portrait of a thinking man as he thinks—and, crucially for Rousseau, as he walks and feels. Each of the ten walks in the *Reveries* is grounded in the everyday, and it is precisely their anecdotal, down-to-earth quality that makes them so appealing. The things Rousseau does, the places he visits, the people he encounters: all these are spurs to creative introspection. It is as Rousseau observes his fellow human beings and even inter-acts with them that he sets about analysing himself and, in so doing, reflecting on fundamental questions about life and human nature: the experience of suffering and death; the search for indi-vidual happiness and inner peace; the need for personal morality; sociability and misanthropy; love of others; the authenticity (or otherwise) of the individual in society. For example, Rousseau's clear-sighted examination in the Sixth Walk of the mental pro-cesses that determine people's behaviour, and particularly his own, begins with his going on one of his familiar walks to the south of Paris, encountering as usual the woman with her stall and crip-pled son, whom he unthinkingly avoids, an instinctive action that suddenly pulls him up short and leads him to analyse the subtle mechanisms of obligation and duty at work in society. The struc-ture of the text is determined by the chance association of ideas as Rousseau's mind wanders in tandem with his feet. In both Montaigne and Rousseau, everyday details and personal examin-ation are the springboard for broader moral reflection.

Not that that springboard necessarily propels the two writers in the same direction, however. On the contrary, it is revealing, for instance, that Rousseau's account in the Second Walk of his acci-dent at the paws of a Great Dane, while echoing in some respects Montaigne's account of his fall off a horse in his chapter 'On Practice' (II. 6), makes him think quite differently from Montaigne: whereas Montaigne's accident prompts him to reflect on, and pre-pare for, death, Rousseau's, paradoxically, makes him feel as if he is being reborn into life (p. 14).

Ultimately, though, what distinguishes Rousseau most clearly from Montaigne, as he carefully reminds us, is that he is writing for himself. In other words, not only does he take himself as his subject, as Montaigne had done; he also takes himself as his own reader. This is what is radically new about the *Reveries*: the text is intended as a means of expression of his own self for his own self. Montaigne had observed in his chapter 'On Repenting' ('Du repentir', III. 2) that 'my book and I go harmoniously forward at the same pace';[10] in Rousseau's hands, by contrast, the writer, the text, and the reader form one, seamless whole. The unintended reader of the published text—for there is no evidence that Rousseau ever envisaged his *Reveries* being published—is thus implicitly constructed as a kind of voyeur. For some readers, that voyeurism is difficult to bear, even repugnant; for many others, however, their response has been, and continues to be, one of intense identification with Rousseau's experience.

It is precisely the power of the *Reveries* to provoke a sometimes visceral reaction in readers that explains the enduring appeal of the text and its discernible influence on generations of creative artists ever since. In the visual arts, Rousseau's depiction of the solitary individual meditating in nature appears to have influenced nineteenth-century portrait painters like Antoine-Jean Gros, whose full-length posthumous portrait of Christine Boyer, wife of Lucien Bonaparte, painted in 1801, shows the young woman as a solitary walker in a dark and mysterious wood, lost in reverie, gazing at the stream flowing past her; and Pierre-Paul Prud'hon, whose large-scale portrait of the Empress Josephine, commissioned in 1805, shows Josephine sitting in the garden at Malmaison, lost in reverie. In twentieth-century art, perhaps the most disturbing echo of Rousseau's text is to be found in the work of the Belgian surrealist painter René Magritte: in his 1926 painting *The Reveries of the Solitary Walker* (*Les Rêveries du promeneur solitaire*), Magritte responds to his mother's suicide in 1912, when he was only thirteen years old, by painting a bowler-hatted man, who was to become the iconic motif of his entire oeuvre and who effectively represents his alter-ego, with his back turned on his dead mother, who lies on a slab in the foreground. The sense of isolation expressed by Rousseau, whose own mother died when he was only

[10] Montaigne, *The Complete Essays*, 909.

a week old, is here translated into the haunting visual image of a profound psychological trauma.

In music, the influential nineteenth-century Hungarian composer and pianist Stephen Heller, who spent most of his life in Paris and described himself as a solitary dreamer, wrote for the piano a series of three *Walks of a Solitary* (*Promenades d'un solitaire*, Op. 78, 80, 89) in the 1850s as well as *Reveries of the Solitary Walker* (*Rêveries du promeneur solitaire*, Op. 101) in 1862. And in 2004, the contemporary London-based Macedonian composer Nikola Kodjabashia called his experimental, classical/jazz crossover album *Reveries of the Solitary Walker*, being inspired by Rousseau's meditative text in writing his nine variations on a traditional Byzantine chant in honour of the Virgin Mary, the seventh of which is entitled 'Seventh Walk'.

But it is on writers that the *Reveries* have exerted the most powerful influence. Writers at the end of the eighteenth and beginning of the nineteenth centuries were particularly inspired by Rousseau's evocation of the relationship between walking and personal freedom. As an early example of this influence, the narrator of John Thelwall's *The Peripatetic* (1793), Sylvanus Theophrastus, echoing Rousseau in and near Paris, goes on walks in and near London, and, pursuing his 'meditations on foot', writes brief chapters about the people and places he encounters along the way, though the satirical tone he adopts strikes a clear contrast with Rousseau's text. William Hazlitt, for his part, who dismissed Thelwall as 'the flattest writer I have ever read . . . tame and trite and tedious . . . a mere drab-coloured suit in the person of the prose writer', wrote an essay on walking, 'On Going on a Journey' (1821), which shows the influence of Rousseau: much of the essay is about the relationship between walking and thinking, and he declares at the outset that solitude is better on a walk: 'I can enjoy society in a room; but out of doors, nature is company for me. I am then never less alone than when alone.' And later in the nineteenth century, in his book *Walden* (1854), the American Henry Thoreau echoes Rousseau's *Reveries* in leaving society in order to find himself in nature, in his case the woods of Massachusetts, where, he says, 'I never found the companion that was so companionable as solitude'.

Rousseau's vision of the walker in nature, and particularly in mountainous landscapes, also had a particularly strong influence on what might be loosely termed Romantic writers. Mary Wollstonecraft's *Letters written in Sweden, Norway and Denmark* (1796) are a remarkable work of travel writing, in which, clearly echoing Rousseau's *Reveries*, she seeks the source of human happiness in the breathtaking grandeur of the Scandinavian landscape, which occasions a series of brilliant reveries, 'mild and enchanting as the first hopes of love', though she subtly reorients her model by insistently engaging with, rather than distancing herself from, society. William Wordsworth, for his part, followed Rousseau more closely still: journeying across the Alps in 1790, his final destination, before heading back down the Rhine, was the Île de St Pierre, the natural paradise Rousseau describes in the Fifth Walk, to which he then alludes in the famous passage on the 'one life' in the peroration to Book 2 of *The Prelude*. This semi-autobiographical, ambulatory poem, which Wordsworth began writing in 1798–9 and in which he was also inspired by Wollstonecraft's *Letters*, includes, in Book 9, the notion of 'spots of time', which echoes Rousseau's remarks about writing and memory in so far as they are, for Wordsworth, past experiences through which he can trace his own development and which continue to resonate with new meanings many years after the events themselves. The intense beauty of Rousseau's Fifth Walk is also evoked in Friedrich Hölderlin's poems 'To the Germans' ('An die Deutschen', 1800), 'Rousseau' (1800), 'The Rhein' ('Der Rhein', 1801), and 'Mnemosyne' (1802), all of which refer to Rousseau drifting in his boat on the middle of the Lac de Bienne, and in Alphonse de Lamartine's beautiful poem 'The Lake' ('Le Lac'), published in his collection *Poetic Meditations* (*Méditations poétiques*, 1820), in which the poet walks alone at the lac du Bourget, recalling a walk there the previous year with his beloved, who is now ill, and asks the lake to hold into eternity the ephemeral trace of their past happiness. A similar attempt to recover the past is found in Gérard de Nerval's remarkable novella *Sylvie* (1853), in which the newly rich narrator leaves Paris and returns to his native Valois region, north of the city, in search of 'places of solitude and reverie': echoing the Ninth Walk, he evokes country customs and festivals; he shares Rousseau's interest in botany, and he even makes a kind of pilgrimage to Ermenonville, where Rousseau died.

The power of reverie also appealed to a number of French novelists at the beginning of the nineteenth century who gave new embodiments to Rousseau's solitary walker in their isolated, introspective, brooding, and anxious characters: Senancour's *Obermann* (1804), Chateaubriand's *René* (1805), and Mme de Staël's *Corinne* (1807) are all important in this respect. In England, meanwhile, Percy Shelley seized on Rousseau the visionary, describing him in a letter to Thomas Hogg of July 1816 as 'the greatest man the world has produced since Milton'. Shelley was a keen reader of the *Reveries*: he set Claire Clairmont, his wife's stepsister, the task of translating part of the text in August 1814; he drew on it as inspiration for the figure of the visionary poet in his poem *Alastor, or The Spirit of Solitude* (1816); and in his contemporaneous essay 'On Life', he describes how 'those who are subject to the state called reverie, feel as if their nature were dissolved into the surrounding universe, or as if the surrounding universe were absorbed into their being'. And in a slightly different vein, and despite being largely dismissive of Rousseau, Thomas De Quincey echoes the *Reveries*, as well as the *Confessions*, in his *Confessions of an English Opium-Eater* (1821), in which he describes how he 'often fell into these reveries upon taking opium' and how, when in the drug's 'divinest state', the opium-eater 'naturally seeks solitude and silence, as indispensable conditions of those trances, or profoundest reveries, which are the crown and consummation of what opium can do for human nature'.

The image that the *Reveries* give of Rousseau as the wandering, observant, solitary man seems to foreshadow the famous *flâneur* of the nineteenth century, but with the crucial difference that the *flâneur* could only exist in the city, detached from the crowds but endlessly intrigued by them, whereas Rousseau wanted nothing to do with them or the urban experience as a whole. Unlike the *flâneur*, who, in Walter Benjamin's famous description of him, goes 'botanizing on the asphalt', and unlike Søren Kierkegaard, who similarly likened to rural botanizing his urban tours around Copenhagen, observing his human subjects, the solitary Rousseau flees the urban in pursuit of the rural: only outside the city, in solitary communion with nature, can Rousseau really be himself. This distinction notwithstanding, it is striking that in 1862 Baudelaire considered giving the title *The Solitary Walker* (*Le Promeneur solitaire*) to what were to become his *Little Prose Poems* (*Petits Poèmes en prose*, 1869), most of which are about the Parisian metropolis, including 'The Double Room' ('La Chambre double'), 'The Crowds' ('Les Foules'), and 'Solitude' ('La Solitude'), which recall the Second and Fifth Walks of Rousseau's *Reveries*, and 'The Old Clown' ('Le Vieux Saltimbanque') and 'The Cake' ('Le Gâteau'), which echo the Ninth. By contrast, the echoes in Fyodor Dostoevsky's *Notes from the Underground* (1864) are more disturbingly ironic: written, in part, as an inspired polemic against Rousseau, the novel has at its heart a 'lazy bones' who makes a career out of his idleness and seeks comfort in a world of fantasy.

The figure of Rousseau the solitary walker, communing with the natural world, has remained important into the twentieth and twenty-first centuries. Rousseau's influence can be seen in the life and work of the German writer and critic W. G. Sebald, for example. In *The Rings of Saturn* (*Die Ringe des Saturn*, 1995), a meditative work blurring the boundaries between fact and fiction, Sebald's unnamed, solitary narrator travels through Suffolk and, from there, back in time. Sebald went on to write an essay on Rousseau in his collection *Lodgings in a Country House* (*Logis in einem Landhaus*, 1998), which also includes a deeply personal and reflective essay on the Swiss writer Robert Walser, entitled *Le Promeneur solitaire*; and in an interview with Arthur Lubow for *The New York Times* shortly before his untimely death in December 2001, he said that, following in Rousseau's footsteps, the Île de St Pierre was the one place where he had felt truly at home. And like Sebald, the contemporary French writer Michel Butor, perhaps best known for his experimental novels of the 1950s, has also followed Rousseau to Switzerland, where, sharing his interest in botany, he has published his *Botanical Wanderings: Sites of Memory* (*Errances botaniques: lieux de mémoire*, 2003), a four-part account of walks in the Alps, offering, like the *Reveries*, a complex reflection on the links between nature and memory, and in which Butor's words are combined with images by the Swiss painter and illustrator Catherine Ernst.

The work of a great prose stylist and a controversial philosopher, the *Reveries* still appeal to modern readers because they are the enduring testimony of an alienated person who wants to know himself, rebel against the forces that constrain him, and live as an autonomous individual. They are the work of a person who is not afraid to lay bare his psychological fragility and human vulnerability. They give a window onto the soul of someone who is different, who does not fit in, an eccentric/ex-centric that cannot—or does not want to—find a place in conventional, supposedly civilized society. Rousseau is thus at once exceptional—*the* solitary walker who is, he says in the Seventh Walk, 'completely at odds with other men' (p. 74)—and exemplary, someone whose life is, as he puts it in the preface to the Neuchâtel edition of the *Confessions*, 'a point of comparison' for everyone else's (p. 648). How he writes, what he writes about, and who and what he is all combine to make Rousseau a writer of his time, of our time, and of all times. As the twentieth-century French novelist François Mauriac pithily observed, referring to Jean-Jacques Rousseau in an appropriately familiar way: 'It is not enough to say that J.-J. is close to us: he is one of us.'

NOTE ON THE TEXT

ROUSSEAU wrote the *Reveries* between September 1776 and
12 April 1778, using as his starting point notes he took on playing
cards while out walking.[1] By the time of his death in Ermenonville,
north of Paris, where he had been staying with the marquis de
Girardin, in July 1778, he had completed a manuscript of the first
seven of the Walks; a separate manuscript contained the last three,
which remained in note form and, in the case of the Tenth Walk,
incomplete. Following Rousseau's death, the marquis de Girardin
sent these manuscripts, together with the playing cards, to
Rousseau's friend and executor Pierre-Alexandre Du Peyrou in
Neuchâtel, who ensured their publication. The *Reveries* were first
published in Geneva in 1782 alongside the first part (Books 1–6)
of the *Confessions*; it is the text of this edition that is given by
Marcel Raymond in his edition for the Bibliothèque de la Pléiade
(Gallimard), which I have used in preparing this translation.

The *Reveries* have long been known in England. The 1782
edition was reviewed as early as June that year in the *Monthly
Review*, which playfully suggested 'sublime ravings' as a possible
translation for the French term 'rêveries'. It nevertheless argued
that the *Reveries* were a more interesting text than the *Confessions*
with which it was published: 'Though they also contain many
insipid and vulgar anecdotes, such as may happen to every bar-
ber's boy who carries home the wig that his master has dressed, yet
they exhibit entertainment of a higher kind . . . that will diminish
the unfavourable impressions, which these *Confessions* may produce.' The *Monthly Review* continued its critique the following
September, quoting at length from the First Walk, 'a rueful ditty'
which, it says, 'seems to have been penned in a feverish fit'; it adds
of Rousseau that 'this honest man laboured, almost from his
cradle to his grave, under a certain *touch* of insanity'. It concluded
that 'the best minds will find nourishment for their virtue, piety,
and taste, in *many* passages of these *Reveries*, which resemble fruits

[1] See the Introduction, above, p. xxi.

and flowers, scattered here and there through a strange and romantic wilderness'.

The first English translation of the *Reveries*, together with a translation of the first part of the *Confessions*, was published in April 1783 in London for J. Bew in Paternoster Row. The *Monthly Review* remained unimpressed the following August: 'The general disapprobation which we expressed for the original, applies with still stronger force to the translation.' The *Critical Review*, by contrast, argued in May 1783 that the *Reveries* 'deserve our attention', though it despaired of the anonymous translation, in which 'the spirit and force of the original are seldom preserved'. The *English Review* for its part offered a tellingly ambivalent response to the text in the following October: noting that Rousseau's belief that he was the victim of a conspiracy 'appears gradually to have impaired his intellects', it nevertheless argued that 'his lamentations, though unmanly and ill-founded, are engaging and eloquent; his grief and expostulations affect his reader with tenderness, and we shut his book under the workings of a mingled sentiment of admiration, displeasure, and sorrow'.

A second English translation appeared in November 1790, published for G. G. J. and J. Robinson and J. Bew, which the *Critical Review* welcomed much more warmly than the first, stating in March 1791 that it must have been undertaken 'by some more competent author' who has translated the text 'with accuracy and fidelity'; it also commented on the magnitude of the challenge: 'To translate Rousseau is a labour of difficulty, it is bending the bow of Ulysses, which few weaker hands can perform.' A further edition of this 1790 translation appeared in 1796. Thereafter the English reader had to wait until 1927, when a translation by John Gould Fletcher, entitled *The Reveries of a Solitary*, was published in London by Routledge in their 'Broadway Library of Eighteenth-Century French Literature' series; this translation was reprinted in 1971 by Burt Franklin in New York. And in 1979 two translations appeared: one by Peter France, published by Penguin, the other by Charles E. Butterworth, published by New York University Press, which was reissued in 2000 in the University Press of New England edition of *The Collected Writings of Rousseau*.

Translating the *Reveries* is indeed a 'labour of difficulty', as the *Critical Review* described it in 1791, because that is precisely what writing was for Rousseau, as he admits in Book 3 of the *Confessions*: 'I have turned some of my periods over and over in my mind for five or six nights before they were ready to be committed to paper' (pp. 111–12). This might seem not to be the case in the *Reveries*, given that Rousseau dismisses his text in the First Walk as 'merely a shapeless account', adding: 'I shall say what I have thought just as it came to me and with as little connection as yesterday's ideas have with those of tomorrow' (p. 8). However, this is not a disorderly text, but rather one shaped by the thought processes of a painstaking writer. The playing cards bear witness to this, with their physical evidence of Rousseau's habit of writing and rewriting, first in pencil, then in ink. At the macro-structural level, each of the Walks is carefully ordered, and so too, at the microstructural level, are all his sentences: they are very often long, elaborate, and sinuous; in them, Rousseau characteristically deploys thought-provoking symmetries and antitheses, evocative repetitions and cadences, and poignant exclamations and interrogations; and through them, he holds in delicate tension a range of different discourses and styles, from the philosophical to the personal, from the elevated to the everyday, and even from the tragic to the comic. The artful complexity and perceptible musicality of Rousseau's prose are part and parcel of who he is: the manner and the matter are as one.

SELECT BIBLIOGRAPHY

Editions

Œuvres complètes, ed. B. Gagnebin and M. Raymond (Paris: Gallimard, 1959–95), 5 vols. The *Reveries* and other autobiographical works are in volume 1.

Les Rêveries du promeneur solitaire, ed. P. Malandain (Paris: Presses Pocket, 1991).

Les Rêveries du promeneur solitaire, ed. E. Leborgne (Paris: Flammarion, 1997).

Rêveries du promeneur solitaire, ed. M. Crogiez (Paris: Librairie générale française, 2001).

Les Rêveries du promeneur solitaire, ed. R. Morrissey (Fasano: Schena, 2003).

Les Rêveries du promeneur solitaire, ed. F. S. Eigeldinger (Paris: Honoré Champion, 2010).

Biography

Cranston, M., *Jean-Jacques: The Early Life and Work of Jean-Jacques Rousseau, 1712–1754* (London: Allen Lane, 1983).

—— *The Noble Savage: Jean-Jacques Rousseau, 1754–1762* (London: Allen Lane, 1991).

—— *The Solitary Self: Jean-Jacques Rousseau in Exile and Adversity* (London: Allen Lane, 1997).

Critical Works

Broome, J. H., *Rousseau: A Study of his Thought* (London: Edward Arnold, 1963).

Davis, M., *The Autobiography of Philosophy: Rousseau's 'The Reveries of the Solitary Walker'* (Lanham, Md.: Rowman & Littlefield, 1999).

Dent, N. J. H., *Rousseau* (Abingdon: Routledge, 2005).

Friedlander, E., *J.-J. Rousseau: An Afterlife of Words* (Cambridge, Mass.: Harvard University Press, 2004).

Grimsley, R., *Rousseau and the Religious Quest* (Oxford: Clarendon Press, 1968).

—— *Jean-Jacques Rousseau: A Study in Self-Awareness*, 2nd edn. (Cardiff: University of Wales Press, 1969).

McFarland, T., *Romanticism and the Heritage of Rousseau* (Oxford: Clarendon Press, 1995).

O'Hagan, T., *Rousseau* (London: Routledge, 1999).

O'Neal, J. C. (ed.), *The Nature of Rousseau's 'Rêveries': Physical, Human, Aesthetic* (Oxford: Voltaire Foundation, 2008).

—— and Mostefai, O. (eds.), *Approaches to Teaching Rousseau's 'Confessions' and 'Reveries of the Solitary Walker'* (New York: Modern Language Association of America, 2003).

Shklar, J., *Men and Citizens: A Study of Rousseau's Social Theory* (Cambridge: Cambridge University Press, 1969).

Starobinski, J., *Jean-Jacques Rousseau: Transparency and Obstruction*, trans. A. Goldhammer (Chicago: University of Chicago Press, 1988).

Williams, D., *Rousseau, 'Les Rêveries du promeneur solitaire'* (London: Grant and Cutler, 1984).

Wokler, R., *Rousseau: A Very Short Introduction* (Oxford: Oxford University Press, 2001).

Further Reading in Oxford World's Classics

De Quincey, Thomas, *The Confessions of an English Opium-Eater*, ed. Grevel Lindop.

Dostoevsky, Fyodor, *Notes from the Underground*, trans. Jane Kentish, ed. Malcolm Jones.

Rousseau, Jean-Jacques, *Confessions*, trans. Angela Scholar, ed. Patrick Coleman.

—— *Discourse on the Origin of Inequality*, trans. Franklin Philip, ed. Patrick Coleman.

—— *The Social Contract*, ed. and trans. Christopher Betts.

Shelley, Percy Bysshe, *The Major Works*, ed. Zachary Leader and Michael O'Neill.

Staël, Madame de, *Corinne*, trans. Sylvia Raphael, ed. John Isbell.

Thoreau, Henry David, *Walden*, ed. Stephen Allen Fender.

Wollstonecraft, Mary, *Letters written in Sweden, Norway and Denmark*, ed. Tone Brekke and John Mee.

Wordsworth, William, *The Major Works*, ed. Stephen Gill.

A CHRONOLOGY OF
JEAN-JACQUES ROUSSEAU

1712   Birth in Geneva, 28 June, of Jean-Jacques, second son of Isaac
        Rousseau, a clockmaker, and his wife Suzanne Bernard; she
        dies on 7 July. He is brought up mainly by his father.

1728   Having been apprenticed to an engraver since 1725, he leaves
        Geneva; he is briefly a convert to Catholicism in Turin and so
        forfeits Genevan citizenship.

1729   At Annecy, he is taken in by Mme de Warens, through whom
        he had been converted; he earns his living through various
        musical, secretarial, and teaching jobs.

1735–8 Liaison with Mme de Warens at her house Les Charmettes.

1742   Largely self-taught, he goes to Paris intending to make a career
        as a musician and composer.

1743–4 Post at French Embassy in Venice under Comte de Montaigu;
        his first direct contact with political life.

1745   Return to Paris; his opera *The Gallant Muses* (*Les Muses galantes*)
        is performed; he meets Thérèse Levasseur who is to be his perma-
        nent companion and the mother of his five children, all left at the
        Paris orphanage; he is friendly with Diderot and the philosopher
        Condillac; secretarial and musical work, including articles on
        music for Diderot and d'Alembert's *Encyclopaedia* (*Encyclopédie*).

1748   Publication of Montesquieu's great work on political theory
        and other subjects, *The Spirit of Laws* (*De l'Esprit des lois*),
        which is to be an important influence on Rousseau's thought
        in *The Social Contract*.

1750   Rousseau gains prize with essay for Dijon Academy competi-
        tion, *Whether the Restoration of the Sciences and the Arts has
        Assisted in the Purification of Morals* (*Si le rétablissement des sci-
        ences et des arts a contribué à épurer les mœurs*), his *First Discourse*.

1752   Success of his opera *The Village Soothsayer* (*Le Devin du village*).

1754   The *Second Discourse*, also for the Academy of Dijon: *On the
        Origin and Foundations of Inequality* (*Sur l'origine et les fonde-
        ments de l'inégalité*), dedicated to the city of Geneva; Rousseau
        makes public return to Geneva and Calvinism.

1755   Publication of the *Second Discourse*, and of Volume V of the *Encyclopaedia*, containing Rousseau's article on *Political Economy* (*Économie politique*). He studies the political writings of the Abbé de Saint-Pierre and begins an all-embracing political work later abandoned.

1757–8   Nebulous love affair with Sophie d'Houdetot; quarrel involving her but mainly with Diderot and other *philosophe* friends.

1758   Publication of *Letter to d'Alembert on Theatre* (*Lettre à d'Alembert sur les spectacles*), which attacks a plan for a theatre at Geneva, desired by Voltaire among others; preparation of *The Social Contract* and other works.

1761   Publication of *Julie, or the New Héloïse* (*Julie ou la Nouvelle Héloïse*), one of the century's best-selling novels; in July, writes to publisher Rey to say that his treatise on politics is ready.

1762   April: publication of *The Social Contract* (*Du Contrat social*) by Rey in Amsterdam; May: publication of *Émile, or On Education* (*Émile ou De l'éducation*) by Duchesne, in Holland and secretly in France. Both books are condemned by the authorities in Paris and Geneva. Rousseau leaves France to take refuge in Yverdon, in Bernese territory, and then (when expelled by the Bern government), in Neuchâtel, governed by the King of Prussia.

1763   Publication of the *Letter to Christophe de Beaumont* (*Lettre à Christophe de Beaumont*), the Archbishop of Paris, answering the latter's criticisms of the religious ideas in *Émile*. Rousseau gives up Genevan citizenship. J.-R. Tronchin attacks *The Social Contract* in his *Letters Written from the Country* (*Lettres écrites de la campagne*).

1764   Rousseau replies to Tronchin in the *Letters written from the Mountain* (*Lettres écrites de la montagne*), also criticizing Genevan institutions. His cause is taken up by the 'Représentants' party in Geneva. He undertakes his *Project for a Constitution for Corsica* (*Projet d'une constitution pour la Corse*); decides to write his *Confessions*.

1765   After difficulties with the Swiss religious authorities and a stone-throwing incident (the 'lapidation de Môtiers'), he returns to Bernese territory, only to be expelled again; he goes to Berlin and Paris, where he is much visited. Voltaire publishes his *Idées républicaines*, in large part a critique of *The Social Contract*.

1766   Rousseau leaves for England at the invitation of David Hume and lives for a while at Wootton in Staffordshire.

1767   After quarrelling with Hume he returns to France incognito to live for three years in the south-east.

1770   He returns to Paris and copies music for a living.

1771   He writes the *Considerations on the Government of Poland* (*Considérations sur le gouvernement de Pologne*) at the invitation of a Polish nobleman, Wielhorski; gives readings of the *Confessions*.

1778   Having written mainly personal works (*Dialogues*; *Reveries of the Solitary Walker*) in his last years, he dies on 2 July at Ermenonville, north of Paris, where he is buried on a lake island.

1782–9 Rousseau's autobiographical works are published posthumously. His late political writings will only be fully published in the nineteenth century.

1794   Rousseau's remains are transported to the Panthéon.

REVERIES OF THE
SOLITARY WALKER

FIRST WALK

So here I am, all alone on this earth, with no brother, neighbour, or friend, and no company but my own. The most sociable and loving of human beings has by common consent been banished by the rest of society. In the refinement of their hatred they have continued to seek out the cruellest forms of torture for my sensitive soul, and they have brutally severed all the ties which bound me to them. I would have loved my fellow men in spite of themselves. Only by ceasing to be men have they succeeded in losing my affection for them. So now they are strangers, persons unknown who mean nothing to me since that is what they wanted. But what about me, cut off from them and from everything else, what am I? This is what remains for me to find out now. Unfortunately this enquiry must be preceded by a brief examination of my current situation. This is something that I must necessarily address first if I am to make the transition from them to me.

I have been in this strange situation for fifteen years or more,* and it still seems as if I must be dreaming. I still imagine that I must be suffering from indigestion, that I must be sleeping badly, and that I am going to wake up and find myself relieved of my pain and back amongst my friends again. Yes, it must be, I must without realizing it have made the leap from being awake to being asleep, or rather from being alive to being dead. Wrenched somehow out of the normal order of things, I have been thrown into an incomprehensible chaos in which I can make out nothing at all, and the more I think about my current situation, the less I understand where I am.

Ah, but how could I have foreseen the fate which awaited me? And how can I make sense of it today, just as I am living through it? Could I ever in my right mind have thought that one day I, the same man that I was then and the same man that I still am now, would appear and be thought of, without the shadow of a doubt, as a monster, a poisoner, and a murderer, that I would become an abomination to the human race and the plaything of the rabble, that the only greeting that passers-by would offer would be to spit on me, and that a whole generation would by common consent delight in burying me alive? When this strange transformation came about, I was taken unawares and was initially thrown into confusion. My distress and indignation plunged me into a frenzy which has taken no less than ten years to subside,* during which time, as I reeled from one error to another, from one mistake to another and from one foolish act to another, my reckless behaviour gave those who were responsible for my fate all the ammunition that they have so skilfully used to determine it once and for all.

For a long time I put up a fight that was as fierce as it was futile. By fighting without cunning, without skill, without deceit, without caution, frankly, openly, impatiently, and angrily, I managed simply to ensnare myself further and constantly gave them new holds over me which they were careful to exploit. Finally realizing that all my efforts were useless and that I was tormenting myself to no avail whatsoever, I took the only remaining course of action left open to me, which was to accept my fate and stop struggling against the inevitable. I have found in this resignation the cure for all my ills through the peace of mind that it gives me and which was incompatible with continually pursuing a struggle that was as agonizing as it was ineffectual.

Another thing has contributed to this peace of mind. In all the refinement of their hatred, my persecutors omitted one technique that they had forgotten about in their animosity, namely to increase by carefully calculated degrees the effects of their hatred so that they could constantly maintain and renew my suffering by always inflicting some new torment upon me. If they had been clever enough to leave me some glimmer of hope, they would still have me in their clutches. They could still have me as their plaything by luring me into some trap and then wounding me deeply by tormenting me once again with my dashed hopes. But they exhausted all their resources in advance: by leaving me with nothing, they have robbed themselves of everything. They have heaped upon me insults, disparagement, mockery, and shame, but these are no more capable of being increased than of being relieved; they are as incapable of making them any worse as I am of escaping them.

They were so eager to reduce me to my most wretched state that the whole of human power, even abetted by all the tricks of hell, could not now add to my wretchedness any further. Physical pain itself, rather than add to my suffering, would actually distract from it. By making me scream out loud, pain would perhaps spare my groans, and the laceration of my body would deflect that of my heart.

What do I have to fear from them now that everything is over? Since they can no longer make things any worse for me, they can no longer frighten me. Anxiety and terror are ills from which they have delivered me for ever: this is still a relief to me. Real ills have little hold over me; I deal easily with those that I actually experience, but not with those that I fear. My fevered imagination adds them together, turns them over and over, draws them out and increases them. The expectation of them tortures me a hundred times more than their actual presence, and the threat of them is far worse than the blow itself. As soon as they happen, the experience of them strips them of their imagined aura and cuts them down to their true size. I then find them much less significant than I had pictured them, and even in the midst of my suffering I still feel relieved. In this state, freed from all further fear and released from the anxiety of hope, habit alone will be sufficient to make more bearable day by day a situation that nothing can worsen, and as my awareness of it is dulled with time, they have no further means of reviving it. This is the good that my persecutors have done me by so immoderately exhausting all the shafts of their hatred with such lack of restraint. They have deprived themselves of their control over me, and from now on I can treat them with derision.

It is still less than two months since a total calm returned to my heart. For a long time I had not been afraid of anything, but I still hoped, and this hope, now cherished, now frustrated, allowed a thousand different passions to trouble me constantly. An event as sad as it was unforeseen has finally wiped out from my heart this last glimmer of hope and has shown me that my earthly fate is irrevocably fixed for evermore.* Since then I have resigned myself completely and have found peace again.

As soon as I began to realize the full scope of the conspiracy, I gave up all idea of restoring myself to favour in the eye of the public; indeed any such favour, being unreciprocated, would now be quite useless to me. However men tried, they would no longer find in me the same person. Given the disdain that they have inspired in me, I would find any dealings with them dull and even burdensome, and I am a hundred times happier on my own than I could ever be living with them. They have torn from my heart all the pleasures of society. These pleasures could never spring up again at my age; it is too late. From now on they can do me good or ill, everything to do with them is indifferent to me; and whatever they may do, my contemporaries will never mean anything to me.

But I was still counting on the future, and I hoped that a better generation, more closely scrutinizing both the judgements made about me by the present one and its conduct towards me, would easily recognize the lies of those who control it and would finally see me as I am. It is this hope that made me write my *Dialogues* and that made me think of a thousand foolish ways of trying to ensure that they survive for posterity.* This hope, though distant, meant that my soul was just as restless as it was when I was still trying to discover one true heart in the present century, and my hopes, which I had vainly discarded, still made me the plaything of the people of today. I have explained in my *Dialogues* what the basis of this hope was. I was wrong. Fortunately I realized this just in time so that I was able to enjoy before my final hour came a period of complete peace and absolute rest. This period began at the time of which I am speaking, and I have reason to believe that it will continue uninterrupted.

Hardly a day goes by without further reflection confirming to me just how wrong I was to count on the public ever changing its mind about me, even at some future date, since it is led in its view of me by guides who constantly succeed one another in the bodies which have taken against me. Individuals may die, but these collective organizations never die. The same passions thrive in them, and their fervent hatred, as immortal as the Devil who inspires it, remains as active as ever. When all my individual enemies are dead, the doctors* and the Oratorians* will still be alive, and even if these two groups were my only persecutors, I can be sure that they will no more leave my memory in peace after my death than they leave me in peace while I am still alive. Perhaps with the passing of time the doctors, whom I really have offended, might be appeased, but the Oratorians, whom I loved, whom I respected, in whom I had complete trust and whom I have never offended, the Oratorians, men of the Church and semi-monks, will remain forever implacable: their own iniquity makes of me a criminal whom their self-love will never forgive, and the public, whose animosity they will always carefully maintain and renew, will be no more placated than they are.

Everything is finished for me on this earth. Neither good nor ill can now be done to me. There is nothing left for me to hope for or fear in this world, and so I am at peace in the depths of the chasm, a poor, unfortunate mortal, but as impassive as God himself.

Everything outside of me is from this day on foreign to me. I no longer have any neighbours, fellow men or brothers in this world. Being on this earth is like being on another planet onto which I have fallen from the one on which I used to live. If I recognize anything at all around me, it is only objects which distress and rend my heart, and I cannot even look at what touches me and what surrounds me without forever seeing something contemptible which angers me or something painful which wounds me. So let me put far from my mind all those vexatious objects which it would be just as painful as it would be pointless for me to grieve over. Alone for the rest of my life, since it is only in myself that I find solace, hope, and peace, it is now my duty and my desire to be concerned solely with myself. It is in this state of mind that I resume the painstaking and sincere self-examination that I formerly called my *Confessions*.* I am devoting my last days to studying myself and to preparing the account of myself which I shall soon have to render.* Let me give myself over entirely to the pleasure of conversing with my soul, for this is the only pleasure that my fellow men cannot take away from me. If by dint of reflecting on my inner feelings I am able to order them better and put right the wrongs that may remain, my meditations will not be entirely in vain, and while I am now good for nothing on this earth, I shall not have entirely wasted my last days. The leisure of my daily walks has often been filled with delightful thoughts which I am sorry to have forgotten. I shall preserve in writing those which come to me in the future: every time I reread them I shall experience the pleasure of them again. I shall forget my misfortunes, my persecutors, and my shame by thinking of the honour my heart had deserved.

These pages will in fact be merely a shapeless account of my reveries. They will often be about me, because a reflective solitary man necessarily thinks about himself a lot. What is more, all the strange ideas which come into my head as I walk will also find their place here. I shall say what I have thought just as it came to me and with as little connection as yesterday's ideas have with those of tomorrow. But a new awareness of my character and my temperament will nevertheless result from an awareness of the feelings and thoughts which feed my mind day by day in the strange state in which I find myself. So these pages may be considered as an appendix to my *Confessions*, but that is not the title I give them, for I no longer feel I have anything to say which is worthy of it. My heart has been purified in the crucible of adversity, and when I examine it carefully I can find hardly a trace of any guilty inclinations. What could I possibly have left to confess now that my heart has been stripped of all worldly affections? I need no more praise myself than blame myself: I am from now on as nothing amongst men, and that is inevitable, for I no longer have any real relationship or keep any kind of company with them. Unable now to do any good which does not turn to ill, or do anything without harming others or myself, abstaining has become my one and only duty, and I fulfil this duty as much as I possibly can. But whereas my body has nothing to do, my soul remains active, still producing feelings and thoughts, and its inner moral life seems even to have increased with the death of all earthly and temporal interests. My body is now nothing more to me than an irritation, an obstacle, and I am already cutting myself free of it as much as I can.

Such an extraordinary situation surely deserves to be examined and described, and it is to this examination that I devote my final days of leisure. To do this successfully I would need to proceed in an ordered and methodical way, but this task is beyond me, and indeed it would distract from my aim, which is to come to an understanding of the sequence of change and effect that has occurred in my soul. I shall in a sense perform on myself the sort of experiments that physicists perform on air to analyse its composition day by day. I shall apply the barometer to my soul, and these experiments, conducted well and repeated time and time again, might yield results as reliable as theirs. But I am not going that far. I shall simply keep a record of the experiments without trying to reduce them to a system. My task is the same as that of Montaigne, but my aim is the exact opposite of his: for he wrote his essays entirely for others, whereas I am writing my reveries entirely for myself.* If, as I hope, I have the same cast of mind when I am very old and as the moment of my departure approaches, reading them will remind me of the pleasure I have in writing them and, by thus reviving the past for me, will double my existence, so to speak. In spite of men I shall still be able to enjoy the delights of company, and, grown decrepit, I shall live with myself in another age, as if living with a younger friend.

When I wrote my earliest *Confessions* and my *Dialogues*, I was constantly concerned with finding ways of keeping them out of the clutches of my persecutors, so that I might be able to pass them on to later generations. That same concern no longer troubles me for this work, for I know it would be in vain, and the desire to be better known by people has died in my heart, leaving me profoundly indifferent to the fate both of my actual writings and of the accounts of my innocence, all of which have perhaps already been destroyed for ever. Let people spy on what I do, let them be alarmed by these pages, seize them, suppress them, falsify them, from now on it is all the same to me. I neither hide them nor show them off. If they are taken away from me during my lifetime, I shall not be deprived of the pleasure of having written them, nor of the memory of what they contain, nor of the solitary meditations which inspired them, the source of which can be extinguished only with my soul. If I had known from the time of my earliest misfortunes not to kick against my fate and to follow the course of action that I am following today, all the efforts of men and all their dreadful machinations would have had no effect on me, and they would have been no more able to trouble my peace of mind with all their plotting than they are able to trouble it from now on with all their triumphs; let them enjoy my humiliation as much as they want, they will not stop me from enjoying my innocence and living the rest of my days in peace in spite of them.

SECOND WALK

HAVING therefore decided that I would describe the habitual state of my soul in this, the strangest position in which any mortal can ever find himself, I could conceive of no simpler or surer way of carrying out my plan than by keeping a faithful record of my solitary walks and the reveries that fill them when I let my mind wander quite freely and my ideas follow their own course unhindered and untroubled. These hours of solitude and meditation are the only time of the day when I am completely myself, without distraction or hindrance, and when I can truly say that I am what nature intended me to be.

I soon felt that I had waited too long to carry out this plan. My imagination, already less vigorous than it once was, no longer bursts into flame in the way it used to upon contemplating the object that inspires it, and I become less intoxicated by the delirium of reverie; now there is more recollection than creation in what my imagination produces, an apathetic listlessness saps all my faculties, and the spirit of life is gradually dying within me; my soul now struggles to spring forward from its decrepit frame, and were it not for the hope I have of the state to which I aspire because I feel entitled to it, I would now exist only through memories. So, if I am to contemplate myself before my decline, I must go back at least a few years to the time when, losing all hope here on earth and finding no more sustenance left on earth for my heart, I gradually became used to feeding it with its own substance and seeking out its nourishment within me.

This practice, which I became aware of all too late, proved so fruitful that it was soon enough to compensate me for everything. The habit of turning in on myself eventually made me insensible to my suffering, and almost made me forget it altogether, and so I learnt through my own experience that the source of true happiness is within us and that it is not within men's ability to make anyone truly wretched who is determined to be happy. For four or five years I had regularly enjoyed the inner delights that loving and gentle souls find in contemplation. These transports of delight and ecstasy which I sometimes experienced when walking on my own were pleasures which I owed to my persecutors: without them, I would never have discovered or known the treasures that I bore within me. Surrounded by such riches, how could one possibly keep a faithful record of them? I wanted to remember so many sweet reveries, but instead of describing them, I relived them. Remembering this state recreates it, and one would soon lose all knowledge of it if one were to cease feeling it altogether.

I experienced this during the walks I went on following my decision to write the sequel to my *Confessions*, in particular during the walk I am about to talk about, in the course of which an unexpected accident interrupted the flow of my ideas and sent them off, for a time, in a quite different direction.

After lunch on Thursday 24 October 1776, I went along the boulevards as far as the rue du Chemin vert,* which I followed up to the heights of Ménilmontant, and from there, taking the paths across the vineyards and meadows, I crossed the delightful countryside that separates Ménilmontant from Charonne, and then I made a detour and came back across the same meadows but by a different path. I enjoyed walking through them, feeling the same pleasure and interest that agreeable landscapes have always given me, and stopping from time to time to look closely at some plants amidst the greenery. I noticed two which I saw quite rarely around Paris but which in this area I found to be growing very abundantly. The first is the *picris hieracioides* of the Compositae family,* and the other the *bupleurum falcatum* of the Umbelliferae family.* This discovery delighted and distracted me for a very long time, until I discovered a plant that is rarer still, particularly on high ground, called the *cerastium aquaticum*,* which, in spite of the accident that happened to me later that day, I later found in a book I had been carrying with me and which I placed in my collection.*

Finally, having examined in detail several other plants I saw which were still in flower and which, in spite of their familiarity, I still enjoyed looking at and cataloguing, I gradually gave up these minute observations in favour of the no less agreeable but more affecting impressions that the scene as a whole made upon me.

A few days earlier the last grapes had been harvested; the walkers from the city had already left; the peasants, too, were leaving the fields, not to return until their winter work began. The country-side, still green and radiant, though some of the leaves had fallen and it was already almost deserted, was the very image of solitude and the onset of winter. Its appearance stirred in me mixed emo-tions of pleasure and sadness which were too similar to my age and my fate for me not to make the comparison. I saw myself in the declining years of an innocent and hapless life, my soul still full of intense feelings and my mind still adorned with a few flowers, though these were already withered by sadness and dried out by care. Alone and abandoned, I could feel the coming chill of the first frosts, and my exhausted imagination no longer peopled my solitude with beings formed after my heart's desires. Sighing, I said to myself: What have I done in this world? I was made to live, and I am dying without having lived. At least I am not to blame, and I shall offer up to the author of my being, if not the good works that I have not been allowed to perform, then at least my tribute of frustrated good intentions, of fine feelings rendered ineffectual, and of a patience that withstood men's scorn. Touched by these reflections, I retraced the different movements of my soul during my youth, during my maturity, since I had been cut off from human society, and during the long isolation in which I am to end my days. I recalled with some fondness all my heart's affec-tions, its attachments which had been so tender and yet so blind, and the ideas—more comforting than they were sad—which had nourished my mind for a number of years, and I prepared myself to remember them clearly enough to be able to describe them with a pleasure that was almost equal to the pleasure of experiencing them in the first place. My afternoon was spent in these untroubled meditations, and I was on my way home, very happy with my day, when in the midst of my reverie I was pulled up short by the event which I shall now recount.

At about six o'clock in the evening, I was walking down from Ménilmontant and was almost opposite the Galant Jardinier* when the people walking ahead of me suddenly stepped aside and I saw a huge Great Dane hurtling towards me, who was bounding along at full speed in front of a carriage* and who did not even have the time, once he had seen me, to slow his pace or change direction. I realized that the only way I could avoid being knocked to the ground was to leap up high enough in the air at just the right moment to let the dog pass beneath me. This idea, which came to me as quick as a flash and which I had no time to reflect on nor to put into action, was my last thought before my accident. I did not feel the impact nor my fall, nor indeed anything else of what happened thereafter until I finally came to.

It was almost night when I regained consciousness. I found myself in the arms of three or four young men who told me what had just happened. The Great Dane, unable to slow down, had run straight into my legs and, overpowering me with his weight and speed, had knocked me over head first: my top jaw, taking the full weight of my body, had struck against a very rough cobblestone, and my fall had been made all the more violent by the fact that, since I was walking downhill, my head ended up lower than my feet.

The carriage to which the dog belonged followed immediately behind him and would have run right over my body had the driver not quickly stopped his horses. This is the account I learned from those who had picked me up and who were still holding me when I came to. The state in which I found myself at that moment is too extraordinary not to be described here.

Night was falling. I saw the sky, a few stars, and a little greenery. This first sensation was a moment of delight. It alone gave me some feeling of myself. In that instant I was born into life, and it seemed to me as if I was filling all the things I saw with my frail existence. Entirely taken up by that moment, I could not remember anything else; I had no clear sense of myself as an individual, nor the slightest idea of what had just happened to me; I did not know who I was nor where I was; I felt neither pain nor fear nor anxiety. I watched my blood flowing as if I were watching a stream, without even thinking that this blood was in any way part of me. Throughout my whole being I felt a wonderful calm with which, whenever I think of it, I can find nothing to compare in the whole realm of known pleasures.

I was asked where I lived; it was impossible for me to say. I asked where I was, and I was told: 'At the Haute Borne';* the answer could just as well have been: 'On Mount Atlas'. I had to ask which country, which town, and which district I was in. But even that was not enough to make me aware of who I was; it took me the entire journey from there to the boulevard to remember where I lived and what my name was. A man whom I had never met before and who was kind enough to walk with me some of the way, on learning that I lived so far away, advised me to take a cab home from the Temple.* I was walking very well, very nimbly, feeling no pain or injury, though I was still spitting lots of blood. But I was shivering with the cold which made my shattered teeth chatter very uncomfortably. When I reached the Temple I thought that, since I was walking without difficulty, I may as well continue on foot rather than run the risk of dying of cold in a cab. Thus I covered the half-league* from the Temple to the rue Plâtrière,* walking without difficulty, avoiding obstacles and vehicles, and choosing which way to go just as I would have done, had I been in perfect health. I arrived home, opened the hidden lock that had been fitted to the street door, climbed the stairs in the dark, and finally reached home, suffering no accident other than my fall and its consequences, of which I was still not even aware.

My wife's cries* when she saw me made me realize that I was more injured than I had thought. I spent the night still not knowing or feeling the full extent of my injuries. This is what I felt and discovered the next day. My top lip was split open on the inside right up to my nose, while the skin on the outside had protected it more and had stopped it from tearing apart completely; four teeth had been knocked in on my top jaw; all the part of my face around my top jaw was extremely swollen and bruised; my right thumb was sprained and very swollen; my left thumb was badly injured; my left arm was sprained; and my left knee was also very swollen, and I was unable to bend it properly because of a big and painful bruise. But in spite of the great knock I had taken, there was nothing broken, not even a tooth: such good fortune was almost a miracle given the fall I had suffered.

This is a very faithful account of my accident. In just a few days the story spread across Paris, but it was changed and disfigured so much that it became quite unrecognizable. I should have known that this would happen; but to it were added so many bizarre circumstances, it was accompanied by so many vague remarks and omissions, and people spoke to me about it in such a ridiculously discreet manner that all these mysteries unnerved me. I have always hated shadows:* they naturally inspire in me a horror that has been in no way diminished by the shadows by which I have been surrounded for so many years. Of all the extraordinary events of this period I will mention only one, but one typical enough to give a sense of the others.

Monsieur Lenoir, the police lieutenant general,* with whom I had never had any dealings, sent his secretary to find out how I was and urgently to offer me favours which, in the circumstances, did not seem to me particularly helpful as I recovered. His secretary did not fail to urge me very insistently to take up these offers, even going so far as to tell me that if I did not trust him, I could write directly to Monsieur Lenoir. His great eagerness and the air of secrecy that he created convinced me that there was, hidden beneath it all, some mystery which I sought in vain to make sense of. This was more than enough to scare me off, especially given the state of agitation which my mind was in on account of my accident and the ensuing fever. I became preoccupied with a thousand worrying and sad conjectures, and I analysed everything that was going on around me in a way which smacked more of the delirium brought on by a fever than of the self-possession of a man who is no longer interested in anything.

Another event succeeded in completely upsetting my peace of mind. Madame d'Ormoy* had been pursuing me for several years, though I had never worked out why. Her pretentious little presents and her frequent pointless and unpleasant visits were a clear enough indication that there was a secret aim behind it all, though they never revealed to me what it was. She had spoken to me about a novel which she wanted to write and present to the Queen.* I had told her what I thought of women writers.* She had given me to understand that the purpose of her project was to restore her fortune, to which end she required a protector; I had nothing to say in reply. She told me subsequently that, having been unable to gain access to the Queen, she had decided to offer her book to the public. There was no longer any point in my giving her advice which she did not seek and which she would not in any case have followed. She had talked about showing me her manuscript before-hand. I asked her not to do so, so she did not.

One fine day during my convalescence I received a copy of her book from her, all printed and even bound,* and I found in the preface such crude praise of me, so clumsily inserted and in such an affected manner that I found it quite unpleasant.* The kind of crude flattery that was expressed there was never a sign of true kindness, about that my heart could not be wrong.

A few days later, Madame d'Ormoy came to see me with her daughter.* She told me that her book was causing a great stir because of a footnote;* I had hardly noticed this note when I flicked through the novel. I reread it once Madame d'Ormoy had left, I examined the way it was phrased, and I believed I found in it the reason for her visits, her honeyed words, and the crude praise in her preface, and I decided that it was all designed to incline the public to attribute the note to me and, consequently, to direct towards me the blame that it could bring upon its author, given the circumstances of its publication.

I had no means of scotching this rumour or the impression which it might create, and all I could do was not to encourage it by allowing Madame d'Ormoy and her daughter to continue their pointless and very public visits. To this end I wrote the mother the following note:

Rousseau, since he does not receive authors, thanks Madame d'Ormoy for her kindnesses and asks her not to honour him with any further visits.

She replied with an apparently polite letter, but one written in the same way as all those written to me in these circumstances. I had barbarously plunged a dagger into her tender heart, and I should realize from the tone of her letter that, since she had such strong and sincere feelings for me, she would not be able to bear this break without dying. So it is that decency and honesty in all things are awful crimes in the world, and I would strike my contemporaries as being wicked and ferocious, even if my only crime in their eyes were that I was not as false and as treacherous as they are.

I had already been out several times and I even walked quite often in the Tuileries,* when I gathered from the surprise shown by many of those who met me that there was yet another story about me of which I was unaware. I finally learned that the rumour going around was that I had died from my fall, and this rumour spread so quickly and so persistently that more than a fortnight after I had learned of it, the King* himself and the Queen spoke of it as if it were a certainty. The *Avignon Courier*, as I was generously informed, in announcing this happy news, did not fail on the occasion to give a foretaste of the tribute of insults and indignities being prepared in my memory for after my death in the form of a funeral oration.*

This news was accompanied by a yet more extraordinary event which I only found out about by chance and of which I have been unable to discover any details. It is that at the same time a subscription was opened to pay for the publication of any manuscripts left in my house. From this I gathered that a collection of fabricated writings had already been prepared precisely in order to attribute them to me immediately after my death: for the idea that any of my real manuscripts would actually be published faithfully was the kind of stupidity which no sensible man could possibly entertain and which fifteen years' experience have guarded me against all too well.

These observations, made one after another and followed by many others which were no less surprising, once more terrified my imagination, which I had thought was deadened, and the dark shadows which were insistently piled up around me revived all the horror that they naturally inspire in me. I exhausted myself trying at length to make sense of it all and trying to understand mysteries which have been made incomprehensible to me. The only unchanging outcome of all these enigmas was the confirmation of all my previous conclusions, namely that, since my own fate and that of my reputation had been fixed by the concerted efforts of the whole of the present generation, nothing I could do could save me from it, since it is utterly impossible for me to entrust anything to future ages without its first being passed through the hands of those that have an interest in suppressing it.

But this time I went further still. The accumulation of so many chance events, the honouring of all my cruellest enemies, favoured, as it were, by fortune, the way in which all those who govern the country, all those who control public opinion, all those in authority, and all those in positions of influence seem to have been hand-picked from among those who have some secret animosity towards me, in order to play their part in the general conspiracy, this universal consensus is too extraordinary to be purely coincidental. One man refusing to be a part of it, one turn of events going against it, or one unforeseen circumstance creating an obstacle to it would have been enough to bring it all crashing down. But every will, every twist of fate, and every change in fortune has consolidated this work of men's hands, and such a striking combination of circumstances, which has something of the miraculous about it, convinces me that its complete success must be written among the eternal decrees. A great number of different observations, both in the past and in the present, convince me of this view so fully that from now on I cannot help regarding as one of Heaven's secrets, impenetrable to human reason, the very plot that hitherto I envisaged only as the fruit of the wickedness of men.

This idea, far from being cruel or heart-wrenching, consoles me, calms me, and helps me to be resigned. I do not go so far as Saint Augustine, who would have been content to be damned, if it had been God's will.* My resignation comes from a less disinterested source, it is true, but for all that it is no less pure and indeed more worthy in my opinion of the perfect Being whom I adore. God is just; he wants me to suffer; and he knows that I am innocent. This is why I am confident: my heart and my reason cry out to me that I shall not be disappointed. So let men and fate have their way; let us learn to suffer without complaining; everything will in the end find its proper place, and sooner or later my turn will come.

THIRD WALK

Growing older, I continue learning.*

SOLON often repeated this line in his old age. In a sense I too could say it in my old age; but the knowledge that experience has given me in the last twenty years* is a very sad one. Ignorance is still preferable. Adversity is without doubt a great teacher, but its lessons come at a cost and often what one gains from them is not worth what one paid for them. Moreover, even before one has acquired all this knowledge from these eleventh-hour lessons, the opportunity to use it has passed. It is in one's youth that one should study wisdom; in one's old age one should practise it. Experience is always instructive, I admit, but it is of use only in the time one has left to live. Is it really the time, when one is about to die, to learn how one should have lived?

Ah, but of what use to me is the knowledge that I have so recently and painfully acquired about my destiny and the passions of those who have shaped it? Understanding men better has only caused me to feel all the more keenly the misery into which they have plunged me, and this understanding, while revealing to me all their traps, has never enabled me to avoid a single one of them. If only I had continued to enjoy that weak-minded yet comforting trust which for so many years made me the prey and plaything of my noisy friends, completely unaware of all their plots while at the same time being enveloped by them. I was their dupe and their victim, it is true, but I thought they loved me, and my heart enjoyed the friendship that they had inspired in me and believed that it was reciprocated. Those sweet illusions have been destroyed. The sad truth that time and reason have revealed to me by making me feel my misfortune has shown me that there is nothing to be done about that misfortune and that the only thing left for me to do is to resign myself to it. So it is that all the experiences of my old age are of no use to me in my current state, nor will they help me in the future.

We enter the race when we are born, we leave it when we die.

What is the point of learning to drive your chariot better when you are at the end of the track? All you have to think about then is how you will leave it. If anything, an old man should learn the art of dying, but this is precisely the kind of study that people of my age are least interested in, indeed they think about anything but that. Old men are more attached to life than children are, and they leave it more grudgingly than young people. This is because, since all their labours have been for this life, they realize, as their life ends, that all their efforts have been in vain. All their concerns, all their riches, all the fruits of their unstinting labours, all this they leave behind when they go. They have not thought about acquiring anything during their lives that they could take with them when they die.

I told myself all this when it was the right time to do so, and if I have been unable to make better use of my reflections, it is not for want of having made them in a timely manner or having carefully mulled them over. Thrown as a child into the maelstrom of the world, I learned from experience at an early age that I was not made to live in it and that in it I would never reach the state for which my heart longed. So, giving up trying to find among men the kind of happiness which I felt I could not find there, my ardent imagination leapt over the whole span of the life that I had barely begun, as if it were unfamiliar territory to me, and sought instead to settle in a quiet resting place where I could make my dwelling.

This feeling, fostered by my childhood education and reinforced throughout my life by the great tissue of miseries and misfortunes with which it has been filled, has at all times prompted me to try to understand the nature and the purpose of being with more interest and determination than I have encountered in any other man. I have seen many men who philosophized much more learnedly than I, but their philosophy was, as it were, external to them. Wanting to be more learned than anyone else, they studied the universe to find out how it was arranged, in the same way as they might have studied some machine that they happened to see, that is, out of pure curiosity. They studied human nature in order to be able to speak learnedly about it, but not in order to know themselves; they worked in order to instruct others, but not in pursuit of their own inner enlightenment. All several of them wanted to do was to write a book, any book, as long as it was well received. Once their book was finished and published, its subject matter was no longer of any interest to them whatsoever, apart from when they wanted others to accept it and when they sought to defend it against attacks, but even then without taking anything from it for their own use and without even worrying about whether it was false or true, so long as it was not challenged. As far as I am concerned, when I have wanted to learn, it has been in order to know myself and not in order to teach; I have always believed that before instructing others, one has first to know enough for oneself, and of all the subjects that I have tried to study in my life surrounded by men, there is hardly one that I would not also have studied if I had been confined on my own, for the rest of my days, on a desert island. What one ought to do depends largely on what one ought to believe, and in everything that is not to do with nature's basic needs, our opinions govern our actions. In accordance with this principle, to which I have always adhered, I have sought often and at length to discover my life's true purpose in order to determine how to live, and I soon became reconciled to my lack of ability to conduct myself skilfully in this world when I realized that here was not the place to seek that purpose.

Born into a moral and pious family and then brought up benevolently by a minister full of wisdom and religion,* I had received from my earliest childhood principles and maxims—some would say prejudices—which have never entirely left me. When still a child and left to my own devices, attracted by kindness, seduced by vanity, deceived by hope, and forced by necessity, I became a Catholic, but I always remained a Christian, and soon my heart, swayed by habit, became sincerely attached to my new religion. The instruction and good example I received from Madame de Warens* confirmed me in this attachment. The rural solitude in which I spent the full flush of my youth and the study of good books, to which I completely devoted myself, reinforced my natural tendency towards affectionate feelings for her and made me almost as devout as Fénelon.* Lonely meditation, the study of nature, and the contemplation of the universe necessarily make a

solitary person strive continually for the author of all things and
seek with a sweet anxiety the purpose of everything he sees and
the cause of everything he feels. When my destiny threw me back
into the torrent of the world, I could not find anything there that
pleased my heart even for a moment. Wherever I went I missed my
sweet freedom and I felt indifference and disgust for anything that
came my way that could have led to fortune and fame. Uncertain
in my troubled desires, I hoped for little, I obtained less, and I felt
in the very glimmers of prosperity that, although I would have
obtained everything I thought I was looking for, I would not have
found that happiness for which my heart longed without knowing
what it was. In this way everything served to cut off my affections
from this world, even before the misfortunes that were to make me
a complete outsider in it. I reached the age of forty, wavering
between poverty and wealth, between wisdom and error, full of
vices born of habit but without any evil inclination in my heart,
living by chance, with no principles governed by my reason, and
careless in my duties, though not neglectful of them, but often
without being fully aware of them.

As a youth I had decided that my reaching the age of forty would
mark the end of my efforts to succeed socially and of all my aspir-
ations. I was determined, once I had reached this age and in whatever position I found myself, no longer to struggle to be released
from it or to spend the rest of my life living from day to day without a thought for the future. When the time came, I had no trouble
in carrying out my plan, and although at that time my fortune
seemed to be about to become more firmly established,* I
renounced it not only without any regrets but also with real pleasure. Freeing myself from all these lures, all these vain hopes, I
devoted myself entirely to the kind of insouciance and peace of
mind that had always been my main preference and most lasting
predilection. I left the world and its vanities, and I renounced all
finery: no more sword, no more watch, no more white stockings,
gold trimmings, or hairdressing, but instead a very simple wig, a
good, solid woollen coat,* and better than all that, I uprooted from
my heart the greed and covetousness that give value to everything
I was leaving behind. I gave up the position I occupied at the time,

a position for which I was in no way suited,* and set about copying music by the page, an occupation for which I had always had a particular liking.

I did not limit my reform to external things. Indeed I felt that this reform demanded another, undoubtedly more painful but also more necessary, namely that of my opinions, and, determined not to go through the whole process twice, I undertook to subject my inner life to a severe examination that would order it for the rest of my days in such a way as I wished to find it at the time of my death.

A great change that had recently taken place in me, a different moral world that was opening up before me,* the irrational judgements of men, whose absurdity I was beginning to feel, though without yet realizing just how much I would fall victim to them, the ever-growing need for something other than literary notoriety, barely a whiff of which had reached me before I was already sickened by it, and finally the desire to follow a less certain road for the rest of my career than that on which I had just spent the better half of it: all this forced me to undertake this great examination which I had felt I needed for a long time. So I undertook it, and I neglected nothing in my power in order to carry it out successfully.

It is from this time that I can date my complete renunciation of the world and that great fondness for solitude that has never left me since. The work that I was undertaking could only be accomplished in absolute isolation; it called for the kind of long and undisturbed meditations that the tumult of society does not allow. That forced me for a time to adopt a different way of life, which I was subsequently so glad to have done that, having since then interrupted it only against my will and for short periods of time, I returned to it most readily and limited myself to it quite easily as soon as I could, and when men later reduced me to living alone, I found that by isolating me in order to make me miserable, they had done more for my happiness than I had been able to do myself.

I set about the work that I had undertaken with a zeal in proportion to both the importance of the task and the need I felt for it. I was living at that time among modern philosophers* who resembled very little the ancient philosophers. Instead of removing my doubts and resolving my uncertainties, they had shaken all the certainties that I thought I had about those things which I considered most important to know: since, as ardent missionaries for atheism and very imperious dogmatists, they could not abide without getting angry anyone daring to think differently from them on any point whatsoever. I had often defended myself quite feebly because I hated debate and was far from adept at it; but I never adopted their wretched doctrine, and this resistance to such intolerant men, who moreover had their own aims in mind, was not the least of the causes that stoked up their animosity towards me.

They had not persuaded me but they had made me anxious. Their arguments had shaken me but without ever convincing me; I could not find a good response to them, but I felt there must be one. I considered myself guilty less of error than of incompetence, and my heart answered them better than my reason.

I finally said to myself: Shall I allow myself to be forever tossed about by the specious arguments of the eloquent whose opinions, which they preach and which they are so keen for others to accept, I am not even sure are their own? Their passions, which determine their opinions and their interest in making people believe this or that, make it impossible to discover what they themselves believe. Can one look for good faith in the leaders of parties? Their philosophy is for others; I need one for myself. Let us look for it with all my strength while there is still time, so that I may have a fixed rule of conduct for the rest of my days. Here I am in my mature years, at the absolute height of my understanding. I am already nearing decline. If I wait any longer, I shall not have all my strength at my disposal in my later deliberations; my intellectual faculties will have lessened their activity, and I shall do less well then what today I can do as well as I ever shall: let us seize this propitious moment; it is the time of my external and material reform, so let it also be the time of my intellectual and moral reform. Let us fix once and for all my opinions and my principles, and let us be for the rest of my life what careful thought will have shown me I should be.

I carried out this plan slowly and in several stages, but with all the effort and attention I could muster. I felt keenly that the tranquillity of the rest of my days and indeed my entire fate depended on it. To begin with I found myself in such a labyrinth of obstacles, difficulties, objections, complexities, and obscurities that, having twenty times been tempted to abandon everything, I was ready to give up my futile research, limit myself in my deliberations to the rules of common prudence, and stop looking for rules in principles which I had such difficulty in disentangling. But even this prudence was so foreign to me and I felt so ill-suited to acquiring it that taking it as my guide would have been akin to searching across high seas and through storms, without a rudder or a compass, for a lighthouse that was barely accessible and that did not show me the way to any port.

I persevered: for the first time in my life I was brave, and it is thanks to this that I was able to bear the horrible destiny that started enveloping me at that time without my having the least suspicion of it. After perhaps the most ardent and sincere research that has ever been undertaken by any mortal, I made up my mind for the rest of my life about all the opinions that it was important for me to have, and even if I may have been wrong in my decisions, I am at least sure that I cannot be reproached for my error, since I did everything I could to avoid it. I do not doubt, it is true, that my childhood prejudices and my heart's secret wishes made the balance swing in the most comforting direction for me. It is difficult to prevent oneself from believing what one so ardently longs for, and who can doubt that the interest one has in accepting or rejecting the judgements of the afterlife determines the faith of most men according to their hopes or their fears? All this was capable of bewitching my judgement, I admit it, but not of undermining my good faith, since I was afraid of getting anything wrong. If the use we make of this life was all that mattered, it was important for me to know so as to be able at least to make the most I possibly could of it while there was still time and not to be a complete dupe. But what I feared most in the world, given the state of mind in which I felt myself to be, was endangering the eternal fate of my soul for the sake of enjoying worldly riches, the value of which has never seemed to me to be very great.

I admit too that I did not always dispel to my own satisfaction all the difficulties that had bewildered me and which our philosophers had so often drummed into my ears. But, determined finally to make up my mind on matters over which human intelligence has such a slight hold and finding on all sides impenetrable mysteries and unanswerable objections, I adopted in each question the opinion which seemed to me the best established and most credible in itself, without worrying about objections which I could not resolve but which were counterbalanced by other, equally strong objections in the opposing system. To adopt a dogmatic tone on these matters would suit only a charlatan; but it is important to have one's own opinion and to choose it with all the maturity of judgement that one can muster. If, in spite of all this, we still fall into error, we cannot reasonably be punished for it since we are not responsible for it. This is the unshakeable principle on which my confidence is founded.

The result of my gruelling research was more or less what I have since written down in the *Profession of Faith of the Savoyard Vicar*,* a work which has been shamefully dishonoured and profaned by the present generation but which one day might cause a revolution among men, if ever good sense and good faith return.

Having remained since then untroubled in the principles which I had adopted after such long and careful meditation, I have made them the unchanging rule of my conduct and my faith and have ceased worrying about the objections which I had been unable to resolve or those which I had not foreseen and which recently arose in my mind from time to time. They have sometimes troubled me but they have never shaken my resolve. I have always said to myself: All these are mere captious arguments and metaphysical subtleties which count as nothing compared to the fundamental principles adopted by my reason, confirmed by my heart, and which all bear the seal of inner assent granted when the passions are silent. In matters so far above human understanding, will an objection that I cannot resolve overturn a whole body of doctrine which is so solid, so coherent, and shaped by so much meditation and care, so well suited to my reason, my heart, and my whole being, and reinforced by the inner assent that I feel to be lacking in all the others? No, vain logic will never destroy the consistency that I perceive between my immortal nature and the constitution of this world and the physical order that I see reigning in it. I find in the corresponding moral order, whose system has been revealed by my research, the support I need to be able to suffer the miseries of this life. In any other system I would live without resources and I would die without hope. I would be the most wretched of creatures. So let us hold fast to that system which alone is able to make me happy in spite of fortune and men.

Do not these deliberations and the conclusion that I drew from them seem to have been inspired by Heaven itself to prepare me for the destiny awaiting me and to enable me to bear it? What would have become of me, what would become of me now, in the awful anguish that awaited me and in the incredible situation to which I am reduced for the rest of my life, if, remaining without any refuge to which I could escape from my implacable persecutors, without any consolation for the ignominy that they make me endure in this world, and without any hope of ever obtaining the justice that was rightly mine, I had been abandoned entirely to the most horrible fate that any mortal on earth has ever suffered? Just as, untroubled in my innocence, I imagined that men would show only respect and goodwill towards me, and just as my frank and trusting heart opened itself up to friends and brothers, the traitors were silently ensnaring me in nets spun in the depths of hell. Caught unawares by the most unforeseen of all misfortunes and the most terrible there can be for a proud soul, dragged through the mud without ever knowing by whom or why, thrown into an abyss of ignominy, and enveloped in horrible darkness through which I could only make out sinister objects, I was brought low by the first shock, and I would never have recovered from the state of total collapse into which this unexpected kind of misfortune threw me, if I had not prepared in advance the strength I needed to pick myself up again when I fell.

It was only after years of anxiety that, finally recovering and beginning to be myself again, I felt the value of the resources that I had prepared in case of adversity. Having made my mind up about all those things on which it was important for me to make a judgement, I saw, when I compared my maxims with the situation I was in, that I accorded far more importance than they actually had to the senseless judgements of men and the trivial events of this short life. Since this life was merely a series of trials, it mattered little of what kind these trials were, so long as they resulted in the effect for which they were designed, and that, consequently, the greater, the more testing, and the more numerous the trials, the more advantageous it was to know how to endure them. All the sharpest pains lose their strength for someone who sees that their recompense is great and sure; and the certainty of this recompense was the principal fruit of my earlier meditations.

It is true that in the midst of the countless injuries and excessive humiliations which I felt being heaped upon me from all sides, moments of anxiety and doubt occasionally shook my hope and disturbed my peace. The powerful objections which I had been unable to resolve then confronted my mind all the more forcefully and completely overwhelmed me at precisely those moments when, overburdened by the weight of my destiny, I was about to fall into despondency. New arguments I heard often resurfaced in my mind in support of those which had already tormented me. Ah! I would then say to myself, the pangs of my heart nearly suffocating me, who will save me from despair if, in the horror of my fate, I now see nothing but fanciful dreams in the consolation that my reason offered me, if, thus destroying its own work, my reason can overturn all the hope and faith that it had given me as support in adversity? What support can illusions give that delude nobody in the world but me? The entire present generation sees only errors and prejudice in the opinions in which I alone find nourishment; it finds truth and clarity in the system opposed to my own; it even seems unable to believe that I have adopted mine in good faith, and even I, while enthusiastically dedicating myself to it, find in it insurmountable difficulties that it is impossible for me to resolve but which do not prevent me from persisting. So am I alone wise, am I alone enlightened among mortals? Is it enough that things suit me for me to believe that they are as they are? Can I put an enlightened trust in appearances which have nothing solid about them in the eyes of the rest of men and which would even seem illusory to me, if my heart did not support my reason? Would it not have been better to fight my persecutors with their own weapons by adopting their maxims than to have held fast to the illusions of my own, vulnerable to their attacks and doing nothing to repel them? I believe myself to be wise but I am merely a dupe, a victim, and a martyr to a pointless error.

How often in these moments of doubt and uncertainty did I come close to giving way to despair. If I had ever been in that state for a whole month, it would have been the end of my life and of me. But these crises, although once quite frequent, were always short-lived, and now, while I am still not completely free of them, they are so rare and so brief that they do not have the same capacity to disturb my peace of mind. These are passing anxieties which have no more effect on my soul than a feather falling into the water has on the course of a river. I felt that to consider again the same points on which I had previously made up my mind was to presuppose that I had new knowledge, a more developed judgement, or a greater zeal for the truth than I had when I conducted my research, and that since none of these was or could be the case with me, I could have no sound reason for preferring opinions which, my being laid low with despair, only tempted me in order to increase my suffering, to opinions I had adopted in the prime of my life, in the full maturity of my mind after the most careful examination, and at a time when the calm of my life left me with no overriding interest other than that of knowing the truth. Today, when my heart is wracked with anguish, my soul weighed down by woe, my imagination frightened, and my head troubled by all the awful mysteries that surround me, today, when all my faculties, weakened by age and anxiety, have lost all their resilience, shall I light-heartedly deprive myself of all the resources that I had prepared for myself and place more trust in my declining reason, which makes me unjustly miserable, than in my full and vigorous reason, compensating me for the ills I suffer undeservedly? No, I am neither wiser nor better informed nor more sincere than I was when I made up my mind on these great questions: I knew full well then the difficulties which today I let trouble me; they did not stop me then, and if there are now new and unforeseen ones, they are but the sophistries of a subtle metaphysics which cannot outweigh the eternal truths which have been accepted at all times and by all wise men, recognized by all nations, and indelibly engraved on the human heart. I knew, as I meditated on these matters, that human understanding, limited by the senses, could not fully comprehend them. I therefore limited myself to what was within my grasp and did not tackle what was beyond it. This course of action was a reasonable one, I adopted it in the past, and kept to it with the approval of my heart and my reason. Why would I renounce it today, when so many powerful motives make me cling to it? What danger do I see in following it? What advantage would I gain in abandoning it? If I were to accept my persecutors' doctrine, would I also have to accept their morality? That morality is the rootless, fruitless morality that they pompously expound in books or in some magnificent action on the stage, without any of it ever penetrating the heart or the reason; or there is also their other, secret, and cruel morality, the hidden doctrine shared by all the initiated, which the other doctrine serves only to mask, which is their sole guide to behaviour and which they have so deftly practised with respect to me. This morality, which is purely offensive, serves no purpose in defence and is good only for attack. Of what use would it be to me in the state to which they have reduced me? My innocence alone supports me in my misfortunes, and how much more miserable would I make myself if, depriving myself of this single but powerful resource, I replaced it with malice? Would I equal them in the art of wronging others, and if I did, which pain of mine would be relieved by the pain I could inflict on them? I would lose my own self-respect and gain nothing in its place.

In this way, reasoning with myself, I succeeded in no longer letting my principles be shaken by specious arguments, insoluble objections, and difficulties which were beyond my grasp and perhaps beyond that of the human mind. My own mind, resting on the most solid foundations I was able to give it, became so used to being settled there, sheltered by my conscience, that no old or new strange doctrine can any longer unsettle it or disturb my peace of mind for a single moment. Sunk in weariness and increasing heaviness of mind, I have forgotten even the arguments on which I based my belief and my maxims, but I shall never forget the conclusions I have drawn from them with the approval of my conscience and my reason, and I shall henceforth hold fast to them. Let all the philosophers come and raise their quibbling objections: they will be wasting their time and effort. For the rest of my life I shall in all things hold fast to the course of action I chose when I was better able to do so.

In this untroubled state of mind, I find not only self-contentment but also the hope and consolation I need in my situation. It is inevitable that a solitude so complete, so permanent, and in itself so sad, the ever-present and ever-active animosity of the entire present generation, and the humiliations which they constantly heap on me should sometimes depress me; shaken hope and discouraging doubts still occasionally return to unsettle my soul and fill it with sadness. It is on such occasions that, incapable of the mental processes necessary to reassure myself, I need to remind myself of my former decisions; the care, the attention, and the sincerity of heart with which I took them then come back to mind and restore my complete confidence. Thus I reject all new ideas as if they were harmful errors which have only a false appearance of truth and which are only fit to disturb my peace of mind.

Confined in this way to the narrow sphere of my former knowledge, I do not have, like Solon, the good fortune to be able to learn as I grow older day by day, and indeed I must avoid the dangerous presumption of wanting to learn what I am now incapable of knowing; but if there are few useful things that I can hope to learn, there is still much I can learn about the virtues necessary for my situation in life. That is why it is time to enrich and adorn my soul with a knowledge that it can take with it when, released from this body that dazzles and blinds it, and seeing the truth unveiled, it perceives the worthlessness of all the knowledge of which our false philosophers are so proud. It will bemoan the time wasted in this life in trying to acquire it. But patience, kindness, resignation, integrity, and impartial justice are treasures that we can take with us and which can make us ever richer, without fear that death itself will ever rob us of their value. It is to this single and useful study that I devote the rest of my old age. I shall be happy if, by the progress I make with myself, I learn to leave life, not better, for that is not possible, but more virtuous than when I entered it.

FOURTH WALK

AMONG the small number of books that I still sometimes read, Plutarch is the author whom I enjoy most and find most useful. He is what I first read as a child, and he will be what I read last in my old age; he is almost the only author whom I have never read without gaining something. The day before yesterday I was reading in his moral works the essay *How to Profit by One's Enemies.** The same day, as I was sorting out some pamphlets that had been sent to me by their authors, I came upon a volume of the abbé Rozier's journal,* on the title page of which he had written these words: *Vitam vero impendenti, Rozier.** Too familiar with these gentlemen and their way with words to be deceived by this, I understood that he had meant, under the air of politeness, to be cruelly ironic: but on what grounds? Why this sarcasm? What could I have done to deserve it? In order to benefit from good Plutarch's lessons, I decided to use my walk the following day to examine myself on the subject of lying, and I set about it firmly committed to the opinion that I had already formed, namely that the *Know thyself* of the Temple at Delphi* was not such an easy maxim to follow as I had believed in my *Confessions*.

The following day, having set off to put this resolution into practice, the first thought that came to me as I started to reflect was of an awful lie* I had told when I was very young, the memory of which has troubled me throughout my life and even now in my old age further afflicts my heart, which is already stricken in so many other ways. This lie, which was a great crime in itself, must have been greater still in terms of its effects, which I have never known about but which my remorse has led me to assume were as cruel as could be. However, considering only my state of mind when I told it, this lie was simply a product of false shame, and far from its resulting from an intention to hurt the girl who was its victim, I can swear in the sight of Heaven that at the very moment when this invincible shame dragged it out of me, I would have gladly given every drop of my blood to have the effect fall on me alone instead. It is an instance of madness that I can only explain by saying what I feel to be true, namely that at that moment my innate timidity got the better of all the wishes of my heart.

The memory of this unfortunate act and the unceasing remorse that it left me inspired in me a horror of lying that should have protected my heart from this vice for the rest of my life. When I adopted my motto, I felt I fully deserved it, and I had no doubt that I was worthy of it when, seeing the abbé Rozier's inscription, I began examining myself more seriously.

As I scrutinized myself more carefully, I was very surprised by the number of things I had invented that I remembered having said as if they were true at the very time when, proud in myself of my love of truth, I sacrificed to that love my security, my best interests, and my own person with a disinterestedness the like of which I have never seen in any other human being.

What surprised me most was that, as I recalled these invented things, I felt no real remorse for them. I, whose horror of falsehood is completely unmatched in my heart by anything else and who would willingly endure torture if the alternative was to avoid it by lying, by what bizarre inconsistency could I thus lie so cheerfully, unnecessarily, and pointlessly, and by what inconceivable contradiction could I do so without feeling the slightest regret, when remorse for a lie has continually afflicted me for fifty years? I have never become inured to my faults; my moral instinct has always guided me well, and my conscience has retained its original integrity, and even if it had changed as it was swayed by my own interests, how could it lose its integrity solely over trivial matters where vice has no excuse, while maintaining its rectitude on those occasions when a man, driven by his passions, can at least excuse himself by his weakness? I realized that the accuracy of the judgement that I had to make about myself in this respect depended on the solution to this problem, and having examined it carefully, this is how I succeeded in explaining it to myself.

I remember having read in a work of philosophy that lying is concealing a truth that one should make known.* It clearly follows from this definition that not telling a truth that one is not obliged to tell is not lying, but if someone who, not being prepared in such circumstances not to tell the truth, says the opposite of the truth, is he lying or not? According to the definition, one could not say that he is lying. For if he gives counterfeit money to a man to whom he owes nothing, he is deceiving that man, certainly, but he is not stealing from him.

There are two questions that need to be examined here, both of them very important. The first is when and how one should tell others the truth, since one does not always have to. The second is if there are cases when one can deceive people innocently. To this second question there are very clear answers, as I know well: the answer is no in books, where the most austere morality costs the author nothing; the answer is yes in society, where the morality of books is seen as twaddle that is impossible to put into practice. So let us leave these authorities who contradict themselves and let us try, following my own principles, to answer these questions for myself.

General and abstract truth is the most precious of all our possessions. Without it man is blind; it is the eye of reason. For through it man learns how to behave, to be what he ought to be, to do what he ought to do, and to strive towards his true purpose. Particular and individual truth is not always a good thing: sometimes it is a bad thing, very often it is an indifferent thing. Those things that it is important for a man to know, and the knowledge of which is necessary to his happiness, are perhaps not very numerous, but however numerous they may be, they are a possession that belongs to him, to which he is right to lay claim wherever he finds it, and of which one cannot deprive him without committing the most iniquitous of all thefts, for this knowledge is one of those possessions that are common to all, and passing it on does not leave the person who gives it in any way bereft.

As for those truths that have no use whatsoever, neither for instruction nor in practical terms, how could they be something that is owed to us, since they are not even a possession? And since property is based only on usefulness, where there is no possible use, there can be no property. One may lay claim to a piece of land, even though it is barren, because at least one can live on it; but whether a trivial fact, entirely unimportant and of no consequence to anybody, is true or false, interests absolutely nobody. Nothing is useless in the moral order nor in the physical order. Nothing can be owed to anybody that is good for nothing: for a thing to be owed to somebody, it must be, or have the potential to be, useful. Thus the truth that is owed is that which concerns justice, and it is to profane the sacred name of truth to apply it to trivial things, the existence of which is a matter of indifference to everyone, and the knowledge of which is totally useless. Truth stripped of any kind of usefulness, even possible usefulness, can therefore not be a thing that is owed to anybody, and consequently anyone who conceals or disguises it is not lying.

But are there any truths so completely sterile as to be utterly useless in every way? This is another issue to which I shall return shortly. In the meantime, let us turn to the second question.

Not saying what is true and saying what is false are two very different things, but they can nevertheless produce the same effect, for this effect is certainly the same whenever it is nil. Whenever the truth is a matter of indifference, so is the opposite error, whence it follows that in such circumstances, a person who deceives by telling the opposite of the truth is no more reprehensible than a person who deceives by not telling the truth, for, as far as useless truths are concerned, error is no worse than ignorance. Whether I believe the sand at the bottom of the sea is white or red is of no more importance to me than not knowing what colour it is. How could one possibly be unjust when one harms nobody, since injustice consists only in the wrong done to others?

But these precipitate answers to my questions cannot give me any sure guidance for practical purposes without their first being sufficiently explained in order to allow them to be applied correctly in all possible cases. For if the duty to tell the truth is founded solely on its usefulness, how can I set myself up as a judge of that usefulness? Very often what does good to one person does harm to another, and private interest is almost always in conflict with public interest. How is one to act in such circumstances? Does what is of use to the absent person have to be sacrificed to that of the person to whom one is speaking? Should the truth that benefits one person but harms another be concealed or declared? Should everything that one has to say be measured solely on the scales of the public good or on those of distributive justice, and can I be sure of knowing all the aspects of the matter well enough to be able to share that knowledge I have purely according to the rules of equity? Moreover, in examining what is owed to others, have I examined sufficiently what one owes to oneself and what one owes to truth itself? If I do no wrong to someone by deceiving them, does it follow that I am doing no wrong to myself, and is it enough never to be unjust in order always to be innocent?

What a lot of thorny issues which it would be easy to get out of by saying to oneself: let us always be truthful, whatever happens. Justice itself lies in the truth of things; lying is always evil, and error is always deceit when one gives what is not true as the rule for what one should do or believe. And whatever effect telling the truth may have, one is always innocent in doing so, because one has added to it nothing of one's own.

But that is to answer the question without actually resolving it. We were not trying to decide whether or not it would be good always to tell the truth, but whether or not one was always equally obliged to do so, and, on the basis of the definition that I was examining, supposing the answer to be no, how to distinguish between those cases where the truth is absolutely necessary and those where one can conceal the truth without injustice and disguise it without lying: for I have found that such cases actually existed. So what we are seeking is a reliable rule for knowing and determining which these cases are.

But where are this rule and the proof of its infallibility to be found . . . ? In all difficult moral questions like this, I have always found it best to be directed by my conscience in answering them, rather than by the insight that comes from my reason. My moral instinct has never deceived me: it has so far remained pure enough in my heart for me to put my trust in it, and if on occasion it falls silent in my actions, in the face of my passions, it reasserts itself over them in my recollections. It is then that I judge myself as severely perhaps as I shall be judged by the supreme judge once this life is over.

To judge men's words by the effects that they have is often to

misjudge them. Apart from the fact that these effects are not always
discernible or easily recognized, they are also as infinitely varied as
the circumstances in which the words are spoken. But it is solely
the intention of the person who speaks them that gives them their
true value and determines their degree of malice or goodness.
Untruthful talk is only lying when there is an intention to deceive,
and the very intention to deceive, far from always being linked to
the intention to do harm, sometimes has quite the opposite purpose. But to make a lie innocent, it is not enough for there to be no
deliberate intention to do harm; rather, it must be certain that the
error into which one is throwing those to whom one is speaking
cannot harm them or anyone else in any way whatsoever. It is rare
and difficult to have this kind of certainty; it is therefore difficult
and rare for a lie to be perfectly innocent. To lie for one's own
advantage is imposture, to lie for the advantage of others is fraud,
and to lie in order to do harm is calumny; this is the worst kind of
lie. To lie without benefit or harm to oneself or to others is not to
lie: it is not a lie, but a fiction.

Fictions which have a moral aim are called apologues or fables,
and since their aim is or should be simply to disguise useful truths
in affecting and pleasing forms, in such cases there is hardly any
attempt to conceal the factual lie, which is simply the disguise of
truth, and the person who tells a fable simply as a fable is in no way
lying.

There are other fictions which are entirely pointless, such as the
majority of tales and novels, which, containing no real instruction,
are designed merely to amuse. Stripped of all moral usefulness,
the true value of these can only be judged in terms of the intention
of the person who invents them, and when he tells them in earnest,
as if they were really true, it is hard to disagree that they are really
lies. However, who has ever worried terribly about such lies, and
who has ever seriously reproached anyone for telling them? If
there is, for example, some moral purpose in *The Temple of Cnidus*,*
it is obscured and undermined by the book's sensual details and
lascivious images. How did the author cover all that with a veneer
of decency? He claimed that his work was the translation of a
Greek manuscript, and he told the story of the discovery of this

manuscript in just such a way as to persuade his readers of the truth of his account. If that is not positively a lie, then I wish someone would tell me what lying is. However, has anyone ever taken it upon himself to treat the author's lie as a crime and to treat him as an impostor because of it?

It is futile to argue that it was merely a joke, that the author, even while making the claim, did not wish to persuade anyone, that in fact he persuaded nobody, and that the public did not doubt for a moment that he was actually the author of the supposedly Greek work that he claimed to have translated. In response I would say that such a pointless joke would have been nothing but a foolish piece of childishness, that a liar is no less a liar when he persuades nobody, and that we must distinguish between the educated public and the hordes of simple and credulous readers who were actually taken in by the story of the manuscript as told by a serious author, apparently in good faith, and who fearlessly drank from an ancient-looking goblet the poison of which they would have at least been wary if it had been presented to them in a modern vessel.

Whether or not these distinctions are to be found in books, they are certainly to be found in the heart of any man who is honest with himself and who does not want to permit himself anything which his conscience could reproach him for. For saying something untrue for one's own advantage is no less of a lie than saying it to harm someone else, even though the lie is less criminal. To give an advantage to someone who should not have it is to undermine order and justice; falsely to attribute to oneself or to someone else an act which may result in praise or blame, or which may be declared innocent or guilty, is to commit an injustice; so, anything which, by dint of running counter to the truth, offends against justice in any way is a lie. That is where I draw the line. But anything which, although running counter to the truth, does not concern justice in any way is but a fiction, and I admit that anyone who reproaches himself for a pure fiction as if it were a lie, has a more delicate conscience than I have.

The lies known as white lies are real lies because deceiving someone to the advantage either of others or of oneself is no less unjust than deceiving someone to harm them. Anyone who praises or blames untruthfully is lying if the person in question is a real person. If the person in question is imaginary, he can say whatever he likes about them without lying, unless he makes judgements concerning the morality of the facts which he invents and makes false judgements, for then, even if he is not lying about facts, he is lying against moral truth, which is a hundred times more respectable than factual truth.

I have seen people who are known in society to be truthful. Their truthfulness expends itself in futile conversations on citing faithfully places, dates, and names, denying any fiction, stating the bare facts, and exaggerating nothing. As long as their own interests are not at stake, they are scrupulously truthful in the account that they give. But when it comes to dealing with some matter that concerns them or narrating some fact that is close to them, they use all their verbal skills to present things in the most favourable light possible, and if a lie is useful to them and even if they refrain from telling it themselves, they contrive to promote it and ensure that it is believed, without it being possible to attribute it directly to them. Such is the will of prudence: farewell, truthfulness.

The man whom I call *truthful* does the exact opposite. In perfectly trivial matters, the truth which the other man respects so much concerns him very little, and he will have few qualms in amusing a gathering with invented facts which give rise to no unfair judgements either for or against anybody living or dead. But any words which produce for somebody advantage or harm, respect or scorn, praise or blame, in spite of justice and truth, are a lie which will never come near his heart, his lips, or his pen. He is resolutely truthful, even when it is not in his own interest to be so, although he rarely makes a point of being so in idle conversation. He is truthful in that he does not seek to deceive anyone, he is as faithful to the truth which accuses him as he is to that which does him credit, and he never deceives for his own advantage or to harm his enemy. The difference, then, between my truthful man and the other is that the man of the world is rigorously faithful to any truth which does not cost him anything, but no more than that, whereas my man never serves truth so faithfully as when he has to lay down his life for its sake.

But, it might be objected, how is it possible to reconcile this leniency with the ardent love of truth which I praise in him? So is this love false because it permits of so much impurity? No, it is pure and true: but it is simply a product of the love of justice and never seeks to be false, even if it is often fantastical. Justice and truth are in his mind two synonyms which he uses interchangeably. The holy truth which his heart adores does not consist of trivial facts and useless names, but of faithfully giving to everyone what is owed to him in things which really pertain to him, in accusations of good or ill, in the awarding of honour or blame, praise or censure. He is not false at the expense of others, because his impartiality prevents him from being so and because he does not want to harm anyone unjustly, nor is he to his own advantage, because his conscience prevents him from being so and because he could not take what does not belong to him. He is above all jealous of his own self-respect; this is the possession that he can least do without, and he would feel a real loss, were he to acquire the respect of others at the expense of his own. Therefore he will have no qualms about sometimes telling lies about trivial matters and he will not believe himself to be lying, but he will never lie to the disadvantage or advantage of others or of himself. In all matters concerning historical truth, in everything concerning the behaviour of men, justice, sociability, or useful knowledge, he will guard himself and others against error as long as it is in his power to do so. In all other matters, a lie is not a lie, according to him. If *The Temple of Cnidus* is a useful work, the story of the Greek manuscript is but a very innocent fiction; it is a reprehensible lie, if the work is dangerous.

Such were my rules of conscience concerning falsehood and truth. My heart followed these rules automatically before my reason had adopted them, and my moral instinct alone put them into practice. The criminal lie of which poor Marion was the victim left me with everlasting remorse which has preserved me for the rest of my life, not only from all lies of this kind, but also from all those which could in any way affect the interests or reputation of others. By making this complete exclusion, I have saved myself from having to weigh up exactly particular rights and wrongs and identify the precise distinctions between harmful lies and white lies; by regarding both as reprehensible, I have ruled them both out equally.

In this as in everything else, my temperament has had a great influence on my principles, or rather on my habits, for I have hardly ever acted according to rules or followed in all things any rule other than that of the promptings of my nature. Never has a premeditated lie come near my mind, and never have I lied to my own advantage; but I have often lied out of shame in order to get myself out of a difficult situation in trivial matters or in matters which concerned me alone, when, having to keep a conversation going, the slowness of my ideas and my dearth of small talk forced me to have recourse to fiction in order to have something to say.* When I am obliged to speak and amusing truths do not spring to mind quickly enough, I tell stories so as not to remain silent; but in making up these stories I am careful as far as possible not to tell lies, that is, to ensure that they do not offend against justice or due truth and that they should simply be fictions that are indifferent to everyone and to me. What I should like to do in telling them is at least to substitute a moral truth for factual truth, that is to depict accurately the human heart's natural affections and to draw from them some useful lesson, to turn them, in short, into moral tales or apologues, but I would need more presence of mind and a greater ease with words than I have to be able to make something instructive out of idle chatter. Conversation, flowing faster than my ideas and forcing me almost always to speak before thinking, has often led me to make stupid and inept remarks which my reason disapproved of and which my heart disowned even before they had passed my lips, but which, spoken before I could apply my judgement, were no longer susceptible to being corrected by its censure.

It is also because of this instinctive and irresistible impulse of my temperament that, in sudden, unforeseen moments, shame and timidity often tear from me lies in which my will has no role but which in a way anticipate it, given the need to respond there and then. The deep impression made on me by the memory of poor Marion may well always stop me from telling those lies which could otherwise be harmful to others, but not those which can help me to get out of a difficult situation when I alone am involved, though these go no less against my conscience and my principles than those which can have an influence on what happens to other people.

I swear to Heaven that if I could instantly withdraw the lie which absolves me and tell the truth which condemns me without disgracing myself still further by recanting, I would do so with all my heart; but the shame of catching myself out in this way still holds me back, and I repent very sincerely of my failing, yet without daring to make amends. An example will explain better what I mean and show that I do not lie out of personal interest or self-love, and still less out of envy or malice, but simply out of embarrassment and false shame, knowing full well sometimes that the lie is known as such and can be of no use to me whatsoever.

Some time ago Monsieur Foulquier* persuaded me, against my custom, to take my wife out to join him and his friend Benoît* for lunch at the restaurant owned by Madame Vacassin, who also ate with us, together with her two daughters. In the middle of the meal, the elder daughter, who had recently married and was pregnant, took it upon herself to ask me abruptly, staring right at me as she did so, if I had any children. I replied, bright red, that I had not had that happiness.* She smiled maliciously at the rest of the group. It was all quite obvious, even to me.

It is clear, first, that this is not the answer I should have given, even if I had wanted to deceive them, since, given the apparent frame of mind of the woman who had put the question to me, I was quite sure that my negative answer would do nothing to change her opinion on the subject. This negative answer was expected, indeed I was provoked into giving it so that she could enjoy the pleasure of making me lie. I was not so stupid as not to realize that. Two minutes later, the answer I should have given came to me in a flash: 'That's a very indiscreet question for a young woman to ask a long-time bachelor.' By saying this, without lying and without having to make an embarrassing confession, I would have had the laughers on my side and taught her a little lesson which would naturally have made her a little less impertinent when questioning me. But I did nothing of the sort: I did not say what I should have said; I said what I should not have said and what could do me no good. So it is clear that neither my judgement nor my will dictated my response and that it was the automatic effect of my embarrassment. In the past I did not get embarrassed in this way and I confessed my faults with more frankness than shame because I was sure that people would see, as I did, deep inside me, those qualities which redeemed them; but the eye of malice wounds and disconcerts me; with my misfortunes I have become more timid, and I have only ever lied out of timidity.

I have never felt more keenly my natural aversion to lying than when I was writing my *Confessions*, for it is there that I could have been frequently and sorely tempted to lie, if I had been so inclined. But far from having passed over or concealed anything that could be used in evidence against me, by a turn of mind which I struggle to understand and which perhaps derives from my antipathy towards all kinds of imitation, I felt more inclined to lie in the opposite way, by accusing myself too severely rather than by excusing myself too indulgently, and my conscience assures me that one day I shall be judged less severely than I judged myself. Yes, I can say and feel with a proud, uplifted soul that in this work I took good faith, truthfulness, and openness as far as, or even further than, any other man has ever done, or at least I believe so; feeling that the good surpassed the bad, it was in my interest to tell the whole truth, and so I told the whole truth.

I never said less than the truth, but sometimes I said more than it, not in the facts themselves, but in the circumstances surrounding them, and this kind of lie was the result of my confused imagination rather than an act of will. I am in fact wrong to call this a lie, since none of these additions was actually a lie. I wrote my *Confessions* when I was already old and disillusioned by the vain pleasures of life, all of which I had tasted and the emptiness of which my heart had felt. I wrote them from memory; my memory often failed me or only provided me with imperfect recollections, and I filled in the gaps with details which I dreamed up to complete those recollections, but which never contradicted them. I enjoyed dwelling on the happy times in my life, and sometimes

I embellished them with ornaments which my fond regrets provided me with. I talked about the things I had forgotten as I thought they must have been, or as they perhaps really had been, but never contradicting what I remembered them to have been. I sometimes invested the truth with exotic charms, but I never replaced it with lies to cover up my vices or to lay claim to virtue.*

If sometimes, thoughtlessly and involuntarily, I concealed my ugly side by painting myself in profile,* these omissions were made up for by other, more bizarre omissions which often made me pass over the good more carefully than the bad. This is a peculiarity of my nature which it is quite excusable for men not to believe, but which, although incredible, is no less real: I often presented what was bad in all its baseness, but I rarely presented what was good in all its worthiness, and I often passed over it completely because it did me too much credit and because it would have looked as if I was praising myself by writing my *Confessions*. I described my early years without boasting about the fine qualities with which my heart was endowed, and indeed I suppressed those facts which drew too much attention to them. I shall recall here two instances from my earliest youth, both of which I remembered when I was writing but which I rejected for the very reason I have just mentioned.

I used to spend nearly every Sunday in Les Pâquis at the home of Monsieur Fazy, who had married one of my aunts and who had a calico works there.* One day I was in the drying room where the calender was, looking at its cast-iron rollers: I liked their shiny appearance, I was tempted to touch them, and I was enjoying running my fingers over the smooth cylinder when Fazy's son, who had got inside the wheel, gave it a half-quarter turn so nimbly that it just caught the ends of my two middle fingers, but that was enough for the ends of them to be crushed and for the two nails to be torn off. I let out a piercing cry and Fazy instantly turned the wheel back, but my nails were still on the cylinder and blood was streaming from my fingers. Fazy cried out in shock, jumped out of the wheel, threw his arms around me, and begged me not to cry so loudly, adding that he would be in serious trouble. At the height of my own pain I was touched by his, I stopped crying, and we went to the pond, where he helped me wash my fingers and stem the flow of blood with moss. In tears he begged me not to blame him for what had happened; I promised him I would not, and I kept my promise so faithfully that, more than twenty years later, nobody knew what had caused me to have two scarred fingers, for so they have always remained. I was confined to my bed for more than three weeks, and for more than two months I was unable to use my hand, and I always claimed that a big stone had fallen on my fingers and crushed them.

> *Magnanima menzogna! or quando è il vero*
> *Si bello che si possa a te preporre?**

I was, however, deeply affected by this accident because of the circumstances in which it happened, since it was when the citizens were due to perform their military exercises, and three other boys of my age and I had formed a group with which, wearing my uniform, I was to take part in the exercises with my district's company. I had the agony of hearing the company drums pass beneath my window with my three friends while I was in bed.

My other story is very similar, though it occurred later in my life.

I was playing a game of mall* at Plain-Palais* with one of my friends, Pleince. We got into a row over the game, we started fighting, and as we fought, he struck me on my bare head with a well-aimed blow of his mallet which, had he been stronger, would have cracked my skull. I instantly fell to the ground. I have never in my life seen anyone so distressed as that poor boy was when he saw the blood flowing through my hair. He thought he had killed me. He flung himself on to me, took me in his arms, and hugged me tightly, weeping and letting out piercing cries. I too embraced him with all my strength, crying like him in a confused state which was not altogether unpleasant. Finally he set about staunching my blood, which was still flowing, and, realizing that our two handkerchiefs were not going to be enough, he took me to his mother, who had a little garden nearby. The good lady nearly fainted when she saw the state I was in. But she was able to retain her strength and tend to my wound, and having washed it thoroughly, she put on it lily flowers soaked in brandy, an excellent vulnerary which is widely used in our country. Her tears and those of her son so touched my heart that for a long time afterwards I looked on her as my mother and on her son as my brother, until eventually I lost sight of them both and gradually forgot them.

I kept this accident as much of a secret as I did the other, and I have had a hundred other similar accidents happen to me during my life which I was not even tempted to talk about in my *Confessions*, so little was I seeking in that work to draw attention to the good that I felt in my character. No, when I have spoken against the truth as I knew it, it has only ever been in trivial matters, and more because of the difficulty I have in speaking or the pleasure I take in writing than out of my own self-interest or for the good or harm it could do to others. And anyone who reads my *Confessions* impartially, if that should ever happen, will feel that the admissions I make in that work are more humiliating and more painful to make than admissions of a greater and yet less shameful wrong would be, which I have not made because I have not committed it.*

It follows from all these reflections that my professed truthfulness is based more on feelings of justice and rectitude than on the reality of things, and that I have followed in practice more the moral dictates of my conscience than abstract notions of truth and falsehood. I have often told lots of stories, but I have very rarely lied. By following these principles I have made myself very vulnerable to criticism from others, but I have done nobody any wrong, and I have not laid claim to more advantage than was owing to me. Only in this way, it seems to me, can truth be a virtue. In all other respects it is for us no more than a metaphysical thing which leads to neither good nor evil.

However, my heart does not feel sufficiently satisfied by these distinctions for me to believe myself entirely beyond reproach. In weighing up so carefully what I owed to others, have I adequately considered what I owed to myself? If one has to be fair to others, one must also be true to oneself, for this is a homage that the respectable man must pay to his own dignity. When my lack of small talk forced me to make up for it by telling harmless stories, I was wrong because one should not debase oneself in order to amuse others, and when, swept along by the pleasure of writing, I embellished real things with made-up ornaments, I was yet more wrong, because to decorate truth with fables is in fact to disfigure it.

But what makes me more unforgivable is the motto I had chosen. This motto obliged me more than all other men to commit myself absolutely to truth, and it was not enough for me always to sacrifice to it my interests and desires; rather, I should also have sacrificed to it my weakness and timid nature. I should have had the courage and the strength always to be truthful, on all occasions, and never to allow fictions or fables to pass my lips or come from my pen which was specifically dedicated to truth. This is what I should have told myself when I adopted this proud motto and repeated to myself over and over again as long as I dared to bear it. My lies were never dictated to me by falsehood; they all came through weakness, though that is a very poor excuse. With a weak soul one may at the very most be able to shun vice, but it is arrogant and reckless to dare to profess great virtues.

Such are the reflections which would probably never have occurred to me, had the abbé Rozier not suggested them to me. It is no doubt too late to make use of them; but at least it is not too late to put right my wrong and to control my will: for this is henceforth all that is in my power to do. In this, then, and in all such things, Solon's maxim is applicable to all ages, and it is never too late to learn, even from one's enemies, to be wise, truthful, modest, and less presumptuous.

FIFTH WALK

Of all the places where I have lived (and I have lived in some charming ones), none has made me so truly happy or left me such sweet regrets as the Île de St Pierre in the middle of the Lac de Bienne.* This little island, which in Neuchâtel is called the Île de la Motte, is not at all well known, even in Switzerland. No traveller, as far as I know, has ever mentioned it. And yet it is very pleasant and wonderfully situated for the happiness of a man who likes to live within defined limits; for, although I am perhaps the only person in the world to whom destiny has decreed that he should live in this way, I cannot believe that I am the only person to have such a natural inclination for it, although I have so far not come across it in anyone else.

The shores of the Lac de Bienne are wilder and more romantic than those of Lake Geneva because the rocks and woods are closer to the water's edge; but they are no less pleasing on the eye. There may be fewer cultivated fields and vineyards and fewer towns and houses, but there is also more natural greenery, there are more meadows and shaded woodland hideaways, and more frequent contrasts and sudden changes in the landscape. Since there are no major roads suitable for carriages on these happy shores, the area is little visited by travellers; but how affecting it is for solitary contemplatives who love to lose themselves altogether in the charms of nature and to meditate in a silence unbroken by any sound other than that of the cry of eagles, occasional birdsong, and the rumbling of streams cascading down the mountains. In the middle of this beautiful, almost circular lake are two small islands, the one inhabited and cultivated, and about half a league* in circumference, the other smaller, deserted, and lying fallow, which one day will end up being destroyed by the constant removal of earth from it to make good the damage done to the big island by waves and storms. Thus it is that the substance of the weak is always used to the advantage of the powerful.

There is only one house on the island, but it is large, pleasant, and comfortable, and it belongs, as the island itself does, to the hospital in Bern and is inhabited by a steward, who lives there with his family and servants. He keeps a well-stocked farmyard, an aviary, and fish ponds. For all its smallness, the island is so varied in soil and position that it has all kinds of places suitable for all sorts of things to be grown. It includes fields, vineyards, woodland, orchards, and rich pastures shaded by trees and lined by shrubs of all varieties, all of which are kept watered by the edges of the lake; a raised terrace, planted with two rows of trees, runs the length of the island, and in the middle of this terrace a pretty summerhouse has been built, where the inhabitants of the neighbouring shores gather for dancing on Sundays during the grape harvest.

It is on this island that I took refuge after the stoning at Môtiers.* I found staying there so charming and I lived in a way so compatible with my nature that, resolving to end my days there, I had no concerns other than that I might not be allowed to carry out this plan, which conflicted with the plan to take me off to England, the first signs of which I was already beginning to detect.* Troubled by these forebodings, I could have wished that this refuge would be turned into a lifelong prison, that I would be confined there for the rest of my life, and that, by being stripped of all power and all hope of ever leaving, I would be forbidden any kind of communication with the mainland so that, not knowing anything of what was going on in the outside world, I might forget its existence and it mine.

I was barely allowed to spend two months on this island,* but I could have spent two years, two centuries, and the whole of eternity there without for a moment becoming bored, even though the only company I had there, apart from my companion, was the steward, his wife, and his servants, who were certainly all very good people and nothing more, but this was precisely what I needed. I consider those two months to be the happiest time in my life, so happy in fact that it would have been enough for me to have lived like that for the whole of my life, without ever feeling in my soul the desire to live in any other state.

So what was this happiness and in what consisted its enjoyment? This would remain a mystery to all the men of this current age,

were I to describe to them the life I led there. Precious *far niente**
was of all the pleasures the first and foremost that I wished to enjoy
in all its sweetness, and everything I did during my stay there was
in fact nothing more than the delicious and necessary pastime of a
man dedicated to idleness.*

The hope that no more would be required of me than to remain
in this isolated place where I had willingly ensnared myself, which
it was impossible for me to leave without help and without being
seen, and where the only communication or correspondence I
could have was through the people surrounding me, this hope in
turn gave me the hope of finishing my days there more peacefully
than I had lived, and the idea that I would have all the time I
needed to settle in meant that, to begin with, I made no attempt to
settle in at all. Having arrived there suddenly, alone and with nothing, I sent in turn for my companion, my books, and my few
belongings, which I had the pleasure of not unpacking, leaving my
boxes and trunks just as they were when they arrived and living in
the home in which I intended to end my days as if it were an inn
that I was supposed to leave the next day. Everything was going so
well as it was that to try to arrange things better would have been
to spoil them. One of my greatest pleasures was above all to leave
my books boxed up and to have no writing desk. When wretched
letters forced me to pick up my pen to write in reply, grumbling I
would borrow the steward's writing desk, and I would quickly
return it in the vain hope of having no further need of it again.
Instead of these sad papers and piles of old books, I filled my room
with flowers and grasses; for I had at that time just become enthu-
siastic about botany, a taste for which I owed to Doctor d'Ivernois*
and which would soon become a passion. No longer wanting to
work, I needed an entertaining pastime that I liked and that would
not require any more effort than an idler could happily devote to
it. I decided to compose a *Flora petrinsularis** and to describe all
the plants on the island, not leaving a single one out, in sufficient
detail to keep me busy for the rest of my days. It is said that a
German once wrote a book about a lemon rind; I could have written one on every grass in the meadows, on every moss in the woods,
and on every lichen covering the rocks; in short, I wanted every

single blade of grass and atom of a plant to be fully described. In order to carry out this fine plan, every morning after breakfast, which we all took together, I would set off, magnifying glass in hand and my copy of *Systema naturae** under my arm, to visit a particular area of the island, which I had divided into small squares for this very purpose, intending to visit them all one after the other in every season. Nothing could be more extraordinary than the great joy and ecstasy I felt every time I observed something about the structure and organization of plants and about the role of the sexual parts in the process of fertilization, which was at that time completely new to me. The distinctions between groups of plants, about which I had previously had no idea, fascinated me as I examined common species and anticipated moving on to rarer ones. The forking of the self-heal's two long stamens, the springiness of those of the nettle and the wall pellitory, the way the fruit of the balsam and the fruit capsule of the box burst open, and the thousand little tricks of fertilization which I was observing for the first time filled me with joy, and I went about asking people if they had seen the horns of the self-heal, just as La Fontaine asked if they had read Habakkuk.* After two or three hours I would come back, laden with an ample harvest, enough to keep me amused at home in the afternoon, should it rain. I spent the rest of the morning with the steward, his wife, and Thérèse, visiting their workers and their harvest, more often than not lending a hand, and often people from Bern who came to see me would find me atop a tall tree with a sack tied round my waist, which I would fill with fruit before lowering to the ground on the end of a rope. My morning exercise and the good mood it invariably put me in made it very pleasant to have a relaxing lunch; but if it went on for too long and the fine weather was enticing me, I could not bear waiting, and while the others were still at the table, I would slip away and get in a boat all alone, which I would row out to the middle of the lake when it was calm, and there, stretching out full-length in the boat, my eyes looking up to the sky, I would let myself float and drift slowly wherever the water took me, sometimes for several hours at a time, plunged in a thousand vague but delightful reveries, which, although they did not have any clear or constant subject, I always found a hundred times preferable to all the sweetest things I had enjoyed in what are known as the pleasures of life.* Often alerted by the setting sun to the fact that it was time to head home, I would find myself so far from the island that I was forced to row with all my strength to get back before nightfall. On other occasions, instead of heading off into the middle of the lake, I enjoyed staying close to the green shores of the island, where the limpid water and cool shade often tempted me to bathe. But one of my most frequent trips was to go from the large island to the small one, to disembark and to spend the afternoon there, sometimes taking very short walks amidst the pussy willows, alder blackthorns, persicarias, and shrubs of all varieties, sometimes setting myself on top of a sandy hillock covered with grass, wild thyme, and flowers, even including sainfoin and clover that had presumably been sown there in the past and that were very suitable for rabbits, which could multiply there in peace, with nothing to fear and without harming anything. I put the idea to the steward, who had male and female rabbits brought over from Neuchâtel, and his wife, one of his sisters, Thérèse, and I went with great ceremony to introduce them onto the little island, where they started breeding before I had left and where they will no doubt have thrived, as long as they have been able to survive the harsh winters. Establishing this little colony was a real celebration. The pilot of the Argonauts* was not prouder than I was as I triumphantly led the people and the rabbits from the large island to the small one, and I was gratified to see that the steward's wife, who had a morbid fear of water and who always got sick in a boat, embarked confidently with me in charge and showed no sign of fear during the crossing.

When the lake was too rough to let me go out in a boat, I would spend my afternoon criss-crossing the island, collecting plants as I went, stopping to sit sometimes in the most beautiful and secluded little spots to dream there at leisure, sometimes on the terraces and hillocks to enjoy the superb and spectacular view over the lake and its shores, on the one side crowned by the nearby mountains, on the other giving way to rich and fertile plains, over which the view extended as far as the distant, bluish mountains.

As evening approached, I would come down from the heights of the island, and I liked to go and sit at the lakeside in some secluded spot on the shingle; there, the sound of the waves and the movement of the water, gripping my senses and ridding my soul of all other agitation, plunged it into a delicious reverie, in the course of which night often fell without my noticing and took me by surprise.* The ebb and flow of the water and its continuous yet constantly varying sound, ever breaking against my ears and my eyes, took the place of the movements inside me that reverie did away with and were enough to make me pleasantly aware of my existence, without my having to take the trouble to think. From time to time there came to mind some slight and brief reflection on the instability of this world, the image of which I saw in the surface of the water: but soon these fragile impressions faded away before the steadiness of the continuous movement which lulled me and which, without my soul actively doing anything, kept me transfixed, so much so that, when time and the agreed signal called me home, I struggled to tear myself away.

After supper, when the evening was fine, we would all go out for a walk on the terrace to breath in the coolness and the air off the lake. We would relax in the summerhouse, laugh, talk, sing some old song which was just as good as the excessively complicated modern ones,* and finally go off to bed, happy with the day that had passed and wishing only for the next day to be similar.

Apart from the unexpected and tiresome visits I sometimes received, this is how I spent my time on this island during my stay there. I wish I knew what was so attractive about it that it should stir in my heart regrets that are so deep, so tender, and so lasting that, fifteen years later,* I still find it impossible to think about this dear place without each time feeling myself transported there by pangs of longing.

I have noticed, however, in the ups and downs of a long life, that it is not the memory of the periods of the sweetest joys and keenest pleasures that draws me and touches me the most. These brief moments of madness and passion, however intense they may be, are, precisely because of their very intensity, only ever scattered points along the line of our life. They are too rare and too fleeting to constitute a proper state of being, and the happiness that my heart longs for is not made up of short-lived moments, but of a simple and lasting state, which has nothing intense about it in itself, but which is all the more charming because it lasts, so much so that it finally offers the height of happiness.

Everything on earth is in a state of constant flux. Nothing keeps the same, fixed shape, and our affections, which are attached to external things, like them necessarily pass away and change. Always beyond or behind us, they remind us of the past which is no longer or anticipate the future which is often not to be: there is nothing solid in them for the heart to become attached to. Thus the pleasure that we enjoy in this world is almost always transitory; I suspect it is impossible to find any lasting happiness at all. Hardly is there a single moment even in our keenest pleasures when our heart can truly say to us: 'If only this moment would last for ever', and how is it possible to give the name happiness to a fleeting state which still leaves our heart anxious and empty, and which makes us regret something beforehand or long for something afterwards?

But if there is a state where the soul can find a position solid enough to allow it to remain there entirely and gather together its whole being, without needing to recall the past or encroach upon the future, where time is nothing to it, where the present lasts for ever, albeit imperceptibly and giving no sign of its passing, with no other feeling of deprivation or enjoyment, pleasure or pain, desire or fear than simply that of our existence, a feeling that completely fills our soul; as long as this state lasts, the person who is in it can call himself happy, not with an imperfect, poor, and relative happiness, such as one finds in the pleasures of life, but with a sufficient, perfect, and full happiness, which leaves in the soul no void needing to be filled. Such is the state in which I often found myself on the Île de St Pierre in my solitary reveries, whether I was lying in my boat as it drifted wherever the water took it, or sitting on the banks of the choppy lake, or elsewhere beside a beautiful river or a stream gurgling over the stones.

What does one enjoy in such a situation? Nothing external to the self, nothing but oneself and one's own existence: as long as

this state lasts, one is self-sufficient like God. The feeling of existence stripped of all other affections is in itself a precious feeling of
contentment and peace which alone would be enough to make this
existence prized and cherished by anyone who could banish all the
sensual and earthly impressions which constantly distract us from
it and upset the joy of it in this world. But most men, being constantly stirred by passion, know little of this state, and, having
only ever experienced it imperfectly and briefly, they have only a
vague and confused idea of it, which gives them no sense of its
charm. It would not even be good in the present circumstances for
them, avidly desiring these sweet ecstasies, to take a dislike to the
active life which their constantly recurring needs impose upon
them. But an unfortunate man who has been cut off from human
society and who can no longer do anything useful or good in this
world either for others or for himself, may find in this state compensation for human joys which neither fortune nor men could
take away from him.

It is true that such compensations cannot be felt by every soul
or in every situation. The heart must be at peace and its calm
untroubled by passion. The person who experiences them must be
suitably disposed to them, as must all the surrounding objects.
There must be neither total calm nor too much agitation, but a
steady and moderate movement with neither jolts nor pauses.
Without movement life is but lethargy. If the movement is irregu-
lar or too violent, it rouses us; by reminding us about the surrounding objects, it destroys the charm of the reverie, tears us out
of ourselves, immediately puts us back beneath the yoke of fortune
and men, and makes us aware of our misfortunes again. Absolute
silence leads to sadness. It offers an image of death. So the help of
a cheerful imagination is necessary and comes quite naturally to
those whom Heaven has blessed with it. The movement which
does not come from outside is created within us on such occasions.
There is less rest, it is true, but it is also more agreeable when light
and pleasant ideas simply brush the surface of the soul, as it were,
without stirring up its depths. One needs just enough of such
ideas to remember oneself while forgetting all one's woes. This
kind of reverie can be experienced wherever one can be quiet, and

I have often thought that in the Bastille, and even in a dungeon with nothing to look at, I could still have dreamed pleasantly.

But admittedly this happened more easily and more pleasantly on a fertile and isolated island, naturally closed off and separated from the rest of the world, where nothing but cheerful images came to me, where nothing recalled sad memories, where the company of the small number of inhabitants was attractive and enjoyable without being so interesting as to take up all my time, where I could, in short, devote myself all day, unhindered and carefree, to the pastimes of my liking or to the most languid idleness. The opportunity was undoubtedly a fine one for a dreamer who, capable of living on agreeable fantasies in the midst of the most unpleasant objects, could take his fill of them at leisure by adding to them everything which actually struck his senses. Emerging from a long and happy reverie and finding myself surrounded by greenery, flowers, and birds, and letting my eyes wander into the distance over the romantic shores bordering a vast stretch of clear and crystalline water, I absorbed into my fictions all these delightful objects, and, finding myself at last gradually brought back to myself and my surroundings, I could not distinguish between fiction and reality, so much did everything combine to make so dear to me the meditative and solitary life I led in that beautiful place. If it could only happen again! If I could only go and end my days on that beloved island, never to leave it again nor see again any inhabitants of the mainland who might remind me of the calamities of all kinds which they have delighted in piling upon me for so many years! They would soon be forgotten for ever; they would not forget me in the same way, of course, but what would it matter to me, so long as they should not be able to come and disturb my peace? Freed from all the earthly passions that the tumult of social life gives rise to, my soul would often soar beyond this atmosphere and would commune before its time with the celestial spirits whose number it hopes soon to increase. Men will, I know, refuse to give me back such a dear refuge, where they did not want to leave me. But at least they will not stop me from transporting myself there every day on the wings of my imagination and tasting for a few hours the same pleasure as if I were still living there. The sweetest thing I would do there would be to dream at my leisure. By dreaming that I am there, am I not doing that very thing? I am in fact doing more: to the attraction of an abstract and monotonous reverie I am able to add charming images which enliven it. The objects of these images often eluded my senses in my ecstasies, and now, the deeper my reverie is, the more vividly it presents them to me. I am often more in their midst and more pleasurably so than I was when I was really there. My misfortune is that as my imagination wanes, this happens with greater difficulty and for shorter periods of time. Alas, it is when one is beginning to leave behind one's mortal body that one is the most hindered by it!

SIXTH WALK

WE have very few instinctive actions whose cause we cannot find in our hearts, if only we know how to look. Yesterday, while walking along the new boulevard* on my way to gather plants along the Bièvre* towards Gentilly,* I took a detour to the right as I approached the Barrière d'Enfer,* and, heading off into the countryside, I took the Fontainebleau road up to the heights alongside this little river. This walk was in itself of no particular interest, but as I remembered that I had several times automatically made the same detour, I sought in myself the reason why, and I could not prevent myself from laughing when I eventually discovered it.

On a corner of the boulevard just beyond the Barrière d'Enfer, a woman sets up a stall every day in summer, selling fruit, tisane,* and bread rolls. This woman has a little boy who is very sweet, but a cripple, and he hobbles along on his crutches, quite cheerfully asking passers-by for money. I had in a sense got to know this little chap; whenever I passed by he would always come and pay me his little compliment, which was always followed by my giving him a little gift. On the first few occasions I was delighted to see him, I gave him money very willingly, and for some time I continued doing so with the same pleasure, most of the time even offering myself the added pleasure of making him chatter and listening to him, which I found to my liking. This pleasure gradually became a habit and thus was somehow transformed into a kind of duty which I soon began to find irksome, above all because of the opening harangue that I was obliged to listen to and during which he never failed to call me Monsieur Rousseau several times to show that he knew me well, which actually showed me, on the contrary, that he knew me no better than those who had taught him. From then on I felt less inclined to go that way, and in the end I instinctively got into the habit of usually making a detour when I approached this gate.

This is what I discovered when I thought about it, for none of this had hitherto been at all clear in my mind. This observation subsequently reminded me of very many others which have convinced me that the real and essential motives of most of my actions are not as clear to me as I had for a long time imagined them to be. I know and feel that doing good is the truest happiness that the human heart can savour; but this happiness was put beyond my reach a long time ago, and it is not in so wretched a destiny as mine that one can possibly hope to place carefully and usefully any one, really good action. Since the greatest concern of those who control my fate has been to ensure that everything for me is merely false and deceptive appearance, any occasion to be virtuous is only ever a bait set for me to entice me into the trap in which they want to ensnare me. I know that; I know that the only good in my power from now on is to refrain from doing anything for fear of unintentionally and unwittingly doing ill.

But there were happier times when, following the impulses of my heart, I could sometimes make another heart happy, and I owe it to myself to acknowledge honourably that every time I enjoyed this pleasure, I found it sweeter than all the rest. This inclination was strong, genuine, and pure, and nothing even deep down within me has ever belied it. However, I often felt the burden of my own good deeds because of the chain of duties they brought with them in their train: then pleasure disappeared, and continuing to offer the same sort of attention which had originally delighted me now became almost unbearably irksome. During my brief periods of prosperity, many people turned to me for help, and doing everything I could for them, I never turned any of them away. But from these early good deeds, which I performed with an overflowing heart, there came chains of successive commitments which I had not foreseen and which I was unable to throw off. My early favours were, in the eyes of those who received them, only the down payment for those that were still to come; and as soon as some unfortunate individual had latched on to me on account of some kindness received, there was from then on no alternative, and that initial, freely given good deed became for him an indefinite right to all those good deeds he might subsequently have need of, and not even my powerlessness was enough to release me. This is how very sweet pleasures were turned into, for me, a succession of onerous obligations.

These chains, however, did not seem to me very heavy as long as I lived in obscurity, unknown by the public. But as soon as my person was exposed by my writings, undoubtedly a serious mistake, albeit one more than made up for by my misfortunes, from that point on I became the one person to whom all the needy or supposedly needy turned, all the tricksters in search of a dupe, and all those who, under the pretext of the great authority they pretended to be attributing to me, wanted to take control of me in some way or another. It was then that I realized that all natural inclinations, including charity itself, once carried or followed in society carelessly and haphazardly, change their nature and often become as harmful as they were originally useful. All these cruel experiences gradually changed my initial inclinations, or rather, confining them at last within their true limits, they taught me to follow less blindly my inclination to do good, when all it did was to further other people's wickedness.

But I do not regret these experiences, since reflecting on them has given me new insights into my knowledge of myself and the real motives for my behaviour on a thousand occasions about which I have so often deluded myself. I came to see that, in order to enjoy doing good, I had to act freely and without constraint, and that in order for me to lose all the pleasure of a good deed, it had only to become a duty for me. From that point on, the weight of obligation turns one of the sweetest joys into a burden, and, as I have said in *Émile* I think, amongst the Turks I would have been a bad husband when the town crier called them to fulfil the duties of their position.*

All this alters considerably the opinion that for a long time I had had of my own virtue, since there is no virtue in following one's inclinations and, when they so lead, in offering oneself the pleasure of doing good. Rather, it consists in overcoming those inclinations when duty requires it in order to do what it tells us to do, and this is what I have been less able to do than any other man in the world. Born sensitive and good, compassionate to the point of weakness and feeling my soul exalted by all things generous, I was by inclination and even by passion humane, benevolent, and charitable, as long as only my heart was touched; I would have been the best and most merciful of men, if I had been the most powerful, and to extinguish in me all desire for vengeance, I would only have needed to be able to avenge myself. I would even have had no difficulty in being fair against my own interests, but I should never have been able to make myself do anything that went against the interests of people who were dear to me. As soon as my duty came into conflict with my heart, the former rarely defeated the latter, unless all I had to do was abstain; on such occasions I was most often strong, but going against my inclinations was always impossible for me. Whether it be men, duty, or even necessity who gives the command, when my heart falls silent, my will remains deaf and I cannot obey. I see the evil threatening me and I let it happen rather than do anything to prevent it. I sometimes make an effort to begin with, but this effort very quickly tires and exhausts me; I am unable to continue. In all imaginable things, what I do not enjoy doing I soon find impossible to do.

And that is not all. Obligation coinciding with my desire is enough to destroy that desire and change it into repugnance, even aversion, if the obligation is too strong, and that is what makes a good deed irksome for me when it is demanded of me, even if I was doing it of my own accord without anyone demanding it of me. A purely voluntary good deed is certainly something that I like to do. But when the beneficiary of it thinks it entitles him to demand more good deeds of me on pain of provoking his hatred if I refuse, and when he insists that I have to be his benefactor for evermore, just because I initially enjoyed being so, from that point on annoyance begins and pleasure subsides. What I do then, when I give in, is weakness and false shame, but good will is no longer part of it, and far from applauding myself for it, I reproach myself in my conscience for doing good unwillingly.

I know that there is a kind of contract, even the most sacred of contracts, between benefactor and beneficiary. It is a kind of society that they form together, more closely knit than that which unites men in general, and if the beneficiary tacitly promises his gratitude, the benefactor likewise agrees to keep showing the other, as long as he remains worthy of it, the same kindness as he has just shown him and to repeat such acts of charity whenever he can and whenever he is required to. These are not explicit conditions, but they are the natural consequences of the relationship that has just been established between them. A person who refuses freely to help someone the first time that person asks them to gives the person whom he has refused no right to complain; but anyone who, in a similar situation, refuses that person the same favour which he had done him in the past, frustrates a hope that he allowed him to form; he disappoints and belies an expectation that he created. In this refusal one feels something unjust and harsher than in the other, but it is no less the product of an independence which the heart loves and which it cannot give up easily. When I pay a debt, it is a duty I am fulfilling; when I give a gift, it is a pleasure I am offering myself. Now, the pleasure of fulfilling one's duties is one which only the habit of virtue can create: those pleasures which come to us directly from nature are not so highly exalted.

After so many unhappy experiences, I have learned to foresee from afar the consequences of following my instinctive inclinations, and I have often abstained from a good deed that I wanted and was able to do for fear of the enslavement to which I would subsequently submit myself if I gave myself over to it unthinkingly. I did not always feel this fear; on the contrary, in my youth I grew fond of others by my own good works, and similarly I often felt that those whom I helped became attached to me more out of gratitude than out of self-interest. But things certainly changed in this respect as in all others as soon as my misfortunes began. From that point on I have lived in a new generation that looked nothing like the old one, and my own feelings for others have suffered from the changes that I found in theirs. The very same people whom I have seen successively in these two very different generations have in a sense assimilated themselves successively first to the one and then to the other. From being truthful and honest to begin with and having become what they are now, they have behaved as everyone else has, and simply because times have changed, men have changed too. Oh, but how could I keep the same feelings for them when I find in them the opposite of what created those feelings? I do not hate them, because I could not hate anybody; but I cannot help but feel the scorn they deserve or show it to them.

Perhaps, without realizing it, I myself have changed more than I should have done. What sort of character could withstand a situation like mine without changing? Convinced by twenty years' experience that all the happy dispositions that nature had put in my heart had been turned, both by my destiny and by those who control it, into something harmful to myself or others, now I can only see a good deed I am asked to do as a trap laid for me, underneath which lurks something bad. I know that, whatever the effect of my good deed may be, I will still be able to take credit for my good intention. Yes, that credit is no doubt still there, but the inner charm is not, and as soon as I do not have this spur, I feel only indifference and coldness within me, and since I am sure that, instead of doing something really useful, I am simply acting the dupe, the combination of my indignant self-love and my reason's denial inspires only opposition and resistance in me, where once, in my natural state, I would have been full of ardour and zeal.

There are some types of adversity which uplift and strengthen the soul, but there are others which weaken and kill it; it is to this latter type that I am prey. If there had been some trace of sin in my soul, this adversity would have made it ferment to excess and driven me delirious; but instead it simply rendered me of no significance. Incapable of doing good either for myself or for others, I abstain from acting at all; and this state, which is innocent only in so far as it is imposed upon me, makes me find a kind of charm in following my natural inclinations fully and without reproach. No doubt I go too far, because I avoid any opportunity to act, even when I see that only good can be done. But, since I am sure that I am not being allowed to see things as they really are, I refrain from judging on the basis of the appearances given to those things, and regardless of how alluring the motives for acting may appear, the very fact that these motives have been left within my grasp is enough to convince me that they are not to be trusted.

I was but a child when destiny seems to have set the first trap, which for a long time made me so prone to fall into all the others. I was born the most trusting of men, and for a whole forty years this trust was never betrayed.* Suddenly plunged into a new order of people and things, I stumbled into a thousand snares without ever noticing a single one of them, and twenty years' experience has hardly been enough to enlighten me about my fate. Once I was convinced that there was nothing but lies and falsehood in the affected protestations of friendship lavished upon me, I quickly went to the other extreme: for once we have left behind our true nature, there is nothing left to constrain us. From then on I grew sick of men, and my own will, coinciding with theirs in this respect, keeps me further removed from them than all their machinations do.

Try as they might, my distaste for them will never turn into aversion. When I think of how they have become dependent on me in their attempt to make me dependent on them, I feel truly sorry for them. If I am not unhappy, then they are, and whenever I reflect on myself, I always find that they are to be pitied. Pride may still form a part of these judgements: I feel myself too much above them to hate them. They may make me feel as much as scorn for them, but never hatred, for I love myself too much to be able to hate anyone. To do so would be to limit and repress my existence, whereas I would prefer to extend it across the whole universe.

I prefer to flee them than hate them. The sight of them strikes my senses and thence my heart with impressions which are made painful for me by a thousand cruel looks; but my distress ends as soon as the object causing it has disappeared. In spite of myself, their presence preoccupies me, but never the memory of them. When I do not see them, they do not exist as far as I am concerned.

They are in fact indifferent to me only in terms of their relations with me; for in their relations with each other, they can still touch me and move me like the characters in a play I might go and see. My moral being would have to be destroyed for justice to become a matter of indifference to me. The spectacle of injustice and wickedness still makes my blood boil with anger; virtuous actions in which I can see no trace of boasting or ostentation always make me tremble with joy and still make me shed sweet tears. But I have to see them and appreciate them for myself; for, given what has happened to me, I would have to be mad to adopt men's judgement on anything or to take anything on trust from anyone.

If my face and features were as completely unknown to men as my character and true nature are, I would have no difficulty in still living amongst them. I could even enjoy their company, as long as I was a perfect stranger to them. Freely following my natural inclinations, I would still love them if they never had anything to do with me. I would display a complete and utterly disinterested benevolence towards them, but without ever forming an attachment to anyone in particular and without taking on the burden of any responsibilities, I would freely and willingly do for them everything that they have so much difficulty in doing, prompted as they are by their self-love and constrained by all their laws.

If I had remained free, unknown, and isolated, as I was meant to be, I would have done only good: for I do not have in my heart the seeds of any harmful passion. If I had been invisible and omnipotent like God, I would have been beneficent and good like him. It is strength and freedom which make excellent men. Weakness and slavery have only ever made wicked men. If I had possessed the ring of Gyges,* it would have released me from being dependent on men and made them dependent on me. I have often wondered, in my castles in the air, what use I would have made of this ring; for in such an instance, power must be closely followed by the temptation to abuse it. Able to satisfy my desires and to do anything at all without anyone being able to deceive me, what might I have desired with some consistency? One thing alone: to see all hearts happy. The sight of public happiness is the one thing that could have touched my heart in a lasting way, and the ardent desire to contribute to it would have been my most constant passion. Always impartially just and unfailingly good, I should also have guarded myself against blind mistrust and implacable hatred; because, seeing men as they are and having no difficulty in reading what is in the depths of their hearts, I would have found few likeable enough to deserve all my affections and few odious enough to deserve all my hatred, and because their very wickedness would have inclined me to pity them, knowing full well the harm they do themselves in seeking to do harm to others. Perhaps in cheerful moments I would have had the childish urge to work some miracles: but completely disinterested in myself and having no other law than my natural inclinations, I would have worked a thousand wonders of forgiveness and fairness for a few acts of severe justice.

As minister of providence and dispenser of its laws according to my power, I would have performed wiser and more useful miracles than those of the Golden Legend* or the tomb of St Medard.*

There is only one point on which the ability to go everywhere unseen could have made me seek out temptations which I would have found difficult to resist, and once I had entered on these wayward paths, who knows where they would have led me? It would suggest a poor understanding of human nature and of myself if I were to flatter myself that these abilities would not have seduced me, or that reason would have stopped me going down this dangerous slope. I was sure of myself in every other respect, but this alone would be my undoing. Someone whose power puts him above man must be above the weaknesses of humanity, otherwise this excess of power will serve only, in effect, to reduce him to beneath his fellow men and beneath what he himself would have been, had he remained the same as them.

All things considered, I think it will be best for me to throw away my magic ring before it makes me do something foolish. If men insist on seeing me as other than I am and if the very sight of me exacerbates their injustice, I need to deprive them of this sight by fleeing them, not by becoming invisible in their midst. It is up to them to hide from me, to conceal their machinations from me, to flee the light of day, and to bury themselves in the ground like moles. As for me, let them see me if they can, so much the better, but that is impossible for them; they will only ever see in my place the J.-J. that they have created for themselves and fashioned to their heart's content, which they can hate at their leisure. So I would be wrong to be upset by the way they see me: I should take no real interest in it, since it is not me that they are actually seeing.

The conclusion I can draw from all these reflections is that I have never really been suited to civil society, where there is nothing but irritation, obligation, and duty, and that my independent nature always made me incapable of the constraints required of anyone who wants to live with men. As long as I act freely, I am good and I do nothing but good; but as soon as I feel the yoke of necessity or men, I become rebellious, or rather, stubborn, and

then I am incapable of doing good.* When I have to do the opposite of what I want to do, I do not do it, whatever happens; I do not
even do what I want to do, because I am weak. I abstain from acting: since my weakness is entirely in terms of action, all my
strength is negative, and all my sins are sins of omission, rarely of
commission.* I have never believed that man's freedom consisted
in doing what he wants to do, but rather in never doing what he
does not want to do, and this is the freedom I have always craved
and often enjoyed and because of which I have most scandalized
my contemporaries. For they, being active, restless, and ambitious,
detesting freedom in others and wanting none of it for themselves,
as long as they can sometimes do what they want to do, or rather
stop other people from doing what they want to do, they go to
great lengths throughout their lives to do what they are loath to do
and will do absolutely anything menial in order to command.
Their wrong was therefore not to cut me off as if I were a useless
member of society, but to banish me as if I were harmful: for I
admit that I have done very little good, but I have never had any
evil intentions in my life, and I doubt if there is any man in the
world who has really done less evil than I have.

SEVENTH WALK

THIS collection of my long reveries has hardly begun, and already I feel that it is coming to an end. Another pastime has taken over from it, absorbs me, and even deprives me of any time for dreaming. I abandon myself to it with an enthusiasm that smacks of the extravagant and that makes me laugh when I think about it; but I abandon myself to it nonetheless because in my current situation, I have no other rule of conduct than always to follow unhindered my natural inclinations. I can do nothing about my fate, all my inclinations are innocent, and since all the judgements of men are henceforth of no significance to me, wisdom itself dictates that in everything that remains within my grasp, I should do whatever I want, be it in public or in private, with no rule other than my own fancy and no constraint other than the little strength that I still have. So here I am with only my hay for food and my botany to occupy me. I was already old when I first gained a superficial knowledge of it in Switzerland from Doctor d'Ivernois, and during my travels I had botanized well enough to gain a decent knowledge of the plant kingdom. But once I was in my sixties and was living a sedentary life in Paris, I began to lose the strength required for lengthy botanizing, and since, moreover, I was busy enough with copying out music not to need any other activity, I had abandoned this pastime which I no longer needed; I had sold my herbarium and my books and was content with sometimes seeing again the common plants that I had found on my walks around Paris. During this time I forgot far more quickly than I had learned it almost all of what little I knew.

Suddenly, already aged sixty-five and having lost both the little memory I had and the strength I had left to run around the countryside, with no guide, no books, no garden, and no herbarium, here I am, once again obsessed with this madness, and even more ardently than I had been the first time I indulged in it; here I am, seriously engaged in the wise plan of learning off by heart the whole of Murray's *Regnum vegetabile** and acquainting myself with every known plant on earth. Unable to buy any books on botany again, I have made it my task to transcribe those lent to me, and, determined to reconstitute a richer herbarium than my first, and until I can put in it all the marine and alpine plants and the trees of the Indies, I am quite happily beginning with pimpernel, chervil, borage, and groundsel; I botanize learnedly at my birdcage, and with every new blade of grass I come across, I contentedly say to myself: 'There's yet another plant.'

I am not trying to justify my decision to follow this whim; I find it very reasonable, since I am persuaded that, in my current situation, indulging in the pastimes that I enjoy is a very wise thing to do, and is even a great virtue: it is a way of preventing any seed of vengeance or hatred from taking root in my heart, and, given my destiny, in order to find a liking for some pastime, I surely need my true nature to have been cleansed of all irascible passions. This is my way of taking revenge on my persecutors: I can think of no crueller way of punishing them than to be happy in spite of them.

Yes, reason without doubt allows me, even requires me, to give myself to any inclination which attracts me and which nothing prevents me from following; but it does not tell me why this inclination attracts me nor what charm I can find in a fruitless study which I pursue without learning anything useful or making any progress and which, old dotard that I am, already decrepit and unwieldy, ungifted and forgetful, takes me back to the exercises of my youth and my schoolboy lessons. Now, this is a bizarre thing that I would like to be able to explain to myself; it seems to me that, once fully explained, it could cast some new light on the self-knowledge which I have devoted my final days of leisure to acquiring.

Sometimes I have thought quite profoundly, but rarely with pleasure and almost always against my will and as if forced to do so: reverie revives and amuses me, thought tires and saddens me; thinking has always been for me a painful and unappealing occupation.* Sometimes my reveries end in meditation, but more often my meditations end in reverie, and during these wanderings, my soul roams and takes flight through the universe on the wings of the imagination in ecstasies that exceed all other pleasures.

As long as I enjoyed this in all its purity, I always found all other occupations dull. But when, having been launched into a literary career by outside forces,* I felt the tiredness caused by intellectual work and the cares created by unfavourable fame, I also felt my sweet reveries languishing and waning at the same time, and soon, being forced in spite of myself to confront my sad situation, only very rarely was I able to rediscover those dear ecstasies which for fifty years had taken the place of fortune and glory for me and which, since I spent nothing on them but time, had made me in my idleness the happiest of mortals.

I even feared in my reveries that my imagination, alarmed by my misfortunes, might finally turn its activity in their direction and that the continual awareness of my sufferings, gradually oppressing my heart, might finally overwhelm me under their weight. In these circumstances, a natural instinct of mine that makes me flee all depressing ideas silenced my imagination and, focusing my attention on the things around me, made me for the first time consider in detail the spectacle of nature, which until then I had hardly ever looked at otherwise than collectively and as a whole.

Trees, bushes, and plants are the adornment and clothing of the earth. Nothing is so sad as the sight of bare, barren countryside that holds up to view nothing but stones, mud, and sand. But brought to life by nature and wearing her wedding dress, amidst flowing water and birdsong, earth offers man, in the harmony of the three kingdoms, a spectacle full of life, interest, and charm, the only spectacle in the world of which his eyes and heart never tire.

The more sensitive the observer's soul, the more he delights in the ecstasy aroused in him by this harmony. On such occasions, a sweet and deep reverie takes hold of his senses, and he loses himself with delicious intoxication in the immensity of this beautiful system with which he feels at one. Then all individual things escape him; everything he sees and feels is in the whole. Some particular circumstances have to restrict his ideas and limit his imagination for him to be able to observe the separate parts of this universe which he was striving to embrace in its entirety.

This is what happened naturally to me when my heart, constricted by distress, gathered and concentrated all its impulses around itself in order to preserve what was left of its warmth which was about to evaporate and die in my ever deepening depression. I wandered aimlessly in the woods and mountains, not daring to think for fear of heightening my pain. My imagination, which rejects all painful things, let my senses yield to the gentle but sweet impressions created by the things around me. My eyes roamed continually from one thing to another, and it was inevitable, given such great variety, that some drew them more and caused them to pause for longer.

I came to enjoy this recreation for the eyes, which in misfortune relaxes, amuses, and distracts the mind and lifts the feeling of pain. The nature of the things adds greatly to this distraction and makes it more charming. Sweet smells, bright colours, and the most elegant of shapes seem to vie for the right to seize our attention. One has only to love pleasure to yield to such delightful sensations, and if the effect is not the same on everyone who is so struck, it is because some lack natural sensibility and most have minds which, too preoccupied with other ideas, only furtively yield to the things which strike their senses.

Something else that also serves to put people of taste off the plant kingdom is the habit of seeing plants only as a source of drugs and medicine.* Theophrastus* had approached them differently, and this philosopher can be thought of as the only botanist of antiquity: for that reason, he is virtually unknown among us; but thanks to a certain Dioscorides,* a great compiler of herbal remedies, and to his commentators, medicine has so seized on plants, all deemed to be medicinal, that people see in them only what is not there to be seen, namely the supposed medicinal virtues that anybody and everybody attributes to them. Nobody imagines that the structure of plants could deserve some attention in its own right; people who spend their lives learnedly classifying shells mock botany as a useless study when it is not combined with what they call the study of properties, that is to say, when one does not abandon the observation of nature, which does not lie and which tells us nothing about any of that, in favour of following entirely the authority of men, who are liars and who tell us lots of things for which we have to take their word, which is itself more often than not based on the authority of others. If you pause in a brightly coloured meadow to examine one by one the flowers with which it shimmers, those who see you, assuming you are a surgeon's assistant, will ask you which plants will cure the mange in children, scabies in men, or glanders in horses. This distasteful prejudice has been partially overcome abroad, and above all in England, thanks to Linnaeus, who has gone some way towards rescuing botany from the schools of pharmacy and returning it to natural history and domestic uses; but in France, where this study has found fewer followers amongst people in polite society, they have remained so barbarous in this respect that a wit from Paris who saw a collector's garden in London, full of rare trees and plants, could only exclaim by way of praise: 'What a fine apothecary's garden.' According to this view, the first apothecary was Adam. For it is hard to imagine a garden with a better stock of plants than the Garden of Eden.

These medicinal ideas are, to be sure, hardly likely to make the study of botany attractive: they make the colour of the meadows and the brilliance of the flowers fade, they dry out the freshness of the woodland, and they make the greenery and shade dull and disagreeable; all the charming and gracious structures of plants are of very little interest to anyone who simply wants to crush them all in a mortar, and it is pointless looking for garlands for shepherdesses amongst the plants used in enemas.

All this pharmacology did not mar my country images: nothing was further removed from them than infusions and poultices. I have often thought, as I looked closely at fields, orchards, woods, and their numerous inhabitants, that the plant kingdom was a food store given by nature to man and animals. But it has never occurred to me to look in it for drugs and remedies. I can see nothing in all its diversity that indicates such a use to me, and nature would have shown us what was available, if it had intended us to use plants in this way, as it did for the food we eat. Indeed, I feel that the pleasure I take in roaming through woodland would be poisoned by the idea of human ailments, if it made me think of fever, stones, gout, and epilepsy. That said, I shall not deny plants the great virtues that are attributed to them; but I shall simply say that, if these virtues are indeed real, the sick are simply being spiteful by continuing to be ill; for of all the illnesses that men give themselves, not one of them can be completely cured by twenty different kinds of plant.

Such views, which always relate everything to our material interest, which make us seek usefulness or remedies everywhere, and which would make us look at the whole of nature with indifference, if we were always well, are ones I have never shared. In this respect I feel I am completely at odds with other men: everything to do with my needs saddens and spoils my thoughts, and I have only ever found real charm in the pleasures of the mind when I have completely lost sight of the interests of my body. Thus, even if I believed in medicine and even if its remedies were agreeable, in using them I would never experience the kind of joy that comes from pure and disinterested contemplation, and my soul could never take flight and soar over nature if I felt it was bound by the ties of my body. Moreover, although I never placed much trust in medicine, I placed a good deal in doctors whom I respected and liked and let rule with complete authority over my carcass. Fifteen years' experience have taught me to my cost; now following once again nothing but the laws of nature, I have regained my original health. Even if the doctors had no other complaints against me, who could be surprised that they hate me? I am the living proof of the vanity of their art and the uselessness of their remedies.

No, nothing personal and nothing to do with the interests of my body can truly concern my soul. My meditations and reveries are never more delightful than when I forget myself. I feel ecstasy and inexpressible rapture when I melt, so to speak, into the system of beings and identify myself with the whole of nature. For as long as men were my brothers, I would make plans for my happiness on earth; since these plans were always formed with reference to the whole, I could only be happy in so far as the public at large was happy, and the only time the idea of individual happiness touched my heart was when I saw my brothers seeking their happiness solely in my misery. So, in order to avoid hating them, I had to flee them; taking refuge in our common mother, in her arms I tried to avoid her children's attacks and I became a solitary or, as they call it, unsociable and misanthropic, because the fiercest solitude seems to me preferable to the society of the wicked, which thrives only on treachery and hatred.

Forced to abstain from thinking for fear of thinking in spite of myself about my misfortunes, forced to repress what remains of a happy but declining imagination, which so many woes could finally scare off completely, and forced to try to forget men who pile ignominy and outrages upon me, for fear that my indignation might finally make me bitter towards them, I am, however, unable to concentrate entirely on myself because my expansive soul seeks, in spite of my best efforts, to extend its feelings and its existence to other beings, and I can no longer, as I once did, plunge headlong into this vast ocean of nature because my weakened and diminished faculties can no longer find any things that are sufficiently distinct, stable, and within my grasp to latch firmly onto and because I no longer feel I have enough strength to swim in the chaos of my former ecstasies. My ideas are now little more than sensations, and the sphere of my understanding is limited to the things closest to me.

Fleeing men, seeking solitude, no longer using my imagination, and thinking still less, yet endowed with a lively temperament that keeps me from falling into listless and melancholy apathy, I began to take an interest in everything around me, and, following a very natural instinct, I preferred the most pleasant things. The mineral kingdom has nothing inherently likeable or attractive about it; its riches, locked up deep inside the earth, seem to have been placed far from the sight of men so as not to appeal to their greed. They are there as a kind of reserve to be used one day as a supplement to those true riches which are more readily in man's grasp and for which he gradually loses his taste as he becomes more corrupt. Then he has to call on dexterity, hard work, and toil to help him in his need; he digs down deep into the bowels of the earth, risking his own life and at the expense of his health, looking in its centre for imaginary gains to replace the real riches that the earth herself freely offered him when he was in a position to enjoy them.

He flees the sun and the light, which he is no longer worthy of seeing; he buries himself alive, and rightly so, since he no longer
deserves to live in the light of day. There, quarries, chasms, forges,
furnaces, and a whole array of anvils, hammers, smoke, and fire
take the place of the sweet images of rustic labour. The haggard
faces of the wretches languishing in the foul vapours of the mines,
blacksmiths covered in soot, and hideous Cyclops are the spectacle
that the mining works present deep down inside the earth, instead
of that of greenery and flowers, azure sky, shepherds in love, and
hearty labourers on the surface.

It is easy, I admit, to go around picking up sand and stones, to
fill your pockets and your cabinet of curiosities with them, and
thus to make yourself look like a naturalist: but those who engage
in, and limit themselves to, these kinds of collections are on the
whole rich, ignorant people who in so doing seek only the pleasure
of showing off what they have collected. In order to gain something useful from studying minerals, one has to be a chemist or a
physicist; one has to perform difficult and costly experiments,
work in laboratories, and spend a great deal of money and time
amidst coal, crucibles, furnaces, retorts, smoke, and suffocating
fumes, always risking one's life and often damaging one's health.
The result of all this wretched and tiring work is usually far less
knowledge than pride: for where is the most mediocre chemist
who does not believe that he has made sense of all the great works
of nature simply because he has discovered, possibly by chance, a
few minor chemical compounds?

The animal kingdom is more within our grasp and certainly
more deserving of study. But does not this study, too, have its own
difficulties, obstacles, annoyances, and trials, above all for a solitary individual who can expect no help from anyone while at play
or at work? How is one to observe, dissect, study, and gain knowledge of the birds in the air, the fish in the water, or the quadrupeds
which are lighter than the wind and stronger than man and which
are no more inclined to come and offer themselves up for my
research than I am to go running after them and subject them to it
by force? I would, then, have to turn to snails, worms, and flies,
and I would spend my life getting out of breath chasing after

butterflies, impaling poor insects, and dissecting mice when I could catch them or the carcasses of animals that I happened to find dead. The study of animals is as nothing without anatomy;* it teaches us how to classify them and distinguish between the different families and species. If I were to study them by their behaviour and characteristics, I would need aviaries, fish-pools, and cages; I would need somehow to force them to stay close to me. I have neither the desire nor the means to keep them in captivity, nor the necessary agility to pursue them as they move about when they are free. So I would have to study them dead, tear them apart, remove their bones, and dig about at will in their palpitating entrails! What an awful place an anatomy theatre is: stinking corpses, oozing and livid flesh, blood, disgusting intestines, awful skeletons, and pestilential fumes! Believe me, that is not the place where J.-J. will go looking for amusement.

Brightly coloured flowers, the varied flora of the meadows, cool shade, streams, woods, and greenery, come and purify my imagination, sullied by all these hideous things. My soul, being dead to all great impulses, can no longer be touched by anything except things that appeal to the senses; sensations are all I have left, and through them alone can pain or pleasure now reach me here on earth. Attracted by the charming things that surround me, I look at them, consider them closely, compare them, and eventually learn to classify them, and all of a sudden, I am as much a botanist as anyone needs to be who wants to study nature with the sole aim of continually finding new reasons for loving it.

I do not seek to educate myself: it is too late for that. In any case, I have never seen any of this science contributing to life's happiness. But I do seek to offer myself pleasant and simple pastimes which I can enjoy effortlessly and which will distract me from my misfortunes. It costs me nothing nor does it take any effort to wander nonchalantly from plant to plant and flower to flower, examining them, comparing their various characteristics, noting their similarities and differences, and, finally, studying how they are organized so as to be able to follow the workings and processes of these living organisms, to discover occasionally their general laws and the reason for, and purpose of, their various structures, and to

give myself over to the pleasure of grateful admiration of the hand
that makes me enjoy all this.

Plants seem to have been scattered profusely over the face of the
earth like the stars in the sky as a means of inviting men, through
the lure of pleasure and curiosity, to study nature; but the stars are
placed far above us: we need to have some basic knowledge, instruments, and machines—so many long ladders enabling us to reach
them and bring them within our grasp. Plants are naturally within
our grasp. They grow beneath our feet and in our hands, so to
speak, and even if their essential parts are so small that sometimes
we cannot see them with the naked eye, the instruments which
make them visible are much easier to use than those used in astron-
omy. Botany is what an idle and lazy solitary studies: a blade and a
magnifying glass are all the equipment he needs to observe plants.
He walks along, wanders freely from one thing to the next, consid-
ers each flower with interest and curiosity, and as soon as he starts
to grasp the laws of their structure, he finds in observing them an
effortless pleasure which is as intense as if it had required of him a
great deal of effort. There is in this idle occupation a charm which
is only felt when the passions are completely calm, but which is
then enough on its own to make life happy and pleasant; but as
soon as we add an element of self-interest or vanity, either to
achieve a certain position or to write books, and as soon as we only
want to learn in order to teach and we only botanize in order to
become an author or a professor, this sweet charm vanishes
entirely: we now see plants simply as the instruments of our passions, we no longer take any real pleasure in studying them, we no
longer want to know but to show that we know, and in the woods,
the world becomes but a stage for us, on which we want to be
admired; or else, limiting ourselves to botany in the study or, at
most, in the garden, instead of studying plants in nature, we concern ourselves only with systems and methods, a subject of endless dispute which does not reveal a single new plant or cast any
real light on natural history or the plant kingdom. This leads to
the hatred and jealousy that rivalry for fame arouses in authors of
botanical works just as much as, and more than, in other scholars.
By changing the nature of this agreeable study, they transplant it

into the middle of towns and academies, where it degenerates no less than exotic plants do in the gardens of collectors.

A quite different cast of mind has made this study a kind of passion for me which fills the emptiness left by those passions I no longer have. I climb up rocks and mountains, I go down deep into valleys and woods in order to escape as far as possible the memory of men and the attacks of the wicked. It seems to me that, in the shade of a forest, I am forgotten, free, and undisturbed, as if I no longer had any enemies or as if the foliage of the woods could protect me from their attacks as it distances them from my memory, and I imagine, in my foolishness, that if I do not think about them, they will not think about me. I find such a great satisfaction in this illusion that I would abandon myself to it completely, if my situation, my weakness, and my needs allowed me to. The deeper the solitude I live in, the more I need something to fill this void, and those things which my imagination denies me or which my memory rejects are made up for by those things that the earth spontaneously produces without any human constraint and sets before my eyes on all sides. The pleasure of going to some isolated spot to look for new plants gives me the added pleasure of escaping from my persecutors, and when I reach places where there is no trace of men, I breathe more freely, as if I were in a refuge where their hate can no longer pursue me.

I shall remember all my life a botanical expedition I made one day over towards La Robella,* a farm belonging to the local judge Clerc.* All alone, I went deep along the winding paths up the mountain, and, passing from wood to wood and rock to rock, I finally reached a refuge that was so hidden that it was wilder than anything I have ever seen in my life. Black fir trees mixed in and all intertwined with huge beech trees, several of which had fallen over with age, formed an impenetrable barrier around this refuge; all that could be seen through the few gaps in this dark wall was sheer rock faces and terrifying chasms which I only dared look into while lying flat on my stomach. From the mountain crevices could be heard the cries of the horned owl, the little owl, and the barn owl; at the same time, a few rare but familiar little birds lightened the horror of this solitude. I found there seven-leaved toothwort,

cyclamen, *nidus avis*,* the large *laserpitium*,* and a few other plants
that delighted and amused me for a long time; but gradually overcome by the strong impression made on me by the things around
me, I forgot about botany and plants, sat down on cushions of
*lycopodium** and mosses, and began dreaming more freely, imagin-
ing that I was in a refuge unknown to the whole universe, where
my persecutors would never be able to unearth me. Soon this reverie was mixed with a feeling of pride. I compared myself to those
great travellers who discover a desert island, and I said compla-
cently to myself: 'I am undoubtedly the first mortal ever to have
reached this place'; I considered myself to be almost another
Columbus. While I was strutting about, caught up in this idea,
I heard not far off a certain clicking noise which I thought I recognized; I listened: the same sound came again and was then repeated
over and over. Surprised and intrigued, I got up, pushed my way
through a thicket of undergrowth in the direction of the noise,
and, set in a little valley twenty yards from the place that I thought
I was the first person to have reached, I saw a stocking factory.

I cannot express the confused and contradictory commotion I
felt in my heart on discovering this. My first instinct was a feeling
of joy at finding myself among human beings again, having thought
myself to be entirely alone; but this instinct, swifter than light-
ning, was soon followed by a more lasting feeling of distress at not
being able, even in the caves of the Alps, to escape the cruel
clutches of those men bent on tormenting me. For I was absolutely
sure that perhaps all but two men at most in that factory were in
on the plot whose self-appointed leader was the minister
Montmollin* and which had its origins further back in the past
still. I quickly banished this gloomy idea, and I ended up laughing
to myself both because of my childish vanity and because of the
comic way in which I had been punished for it.

But after all, who would ever have expected to find a factory in
a chasm? Switzerland is the only country in the world to offer this
mixture of wild nature and human industry. The whole of
Switzerland is, as it were, but one big city, whose wide, long streets,
longer than the rue St Antoine,* are planted with forests and cut
across by mountains, and whose scattered and isolated houses are

only connected with one another by English landscape gardens. With this in mind, I remembered another botanical expedition that Du Peyrou,* d'Escherny,* colonel Pury,* judge Clerc, and I had made some time ago on the Chasseron mountain, from the summit of which can be seen seven lakes. We were told that there was only one house on the mountain, and we would surely never have guessed the profession of the person living there, had we not also been told that he was a bookseller, and indeed that he was doing a very good trade in the region. It seems to me that a single fact of this kind gives a better idea of Switzerland than all the travel accounts put together.

Here is another fact of more or less the same kind which gives an equally good idea of a very different people. During my stay in Grenoble,* I often went on short botanical trips outside the town with Monsieur Bovier,* a local lawyer, not because he liked or knew about botany, but because, since he had appointed himself my bodyguard, he insisted as far as possible on accompanying me wherever I went. One day we were walking by the Isère* in a place full of buckthorns. I saw some ripe berries on the bushes, was curious enough to try them, and, finding their slightly acidic taste very pleasant, started eating them to revive me; Monsieur Bovier stood beside me, neither doing likewise nor saying a word. One of his friends came by and, seeing me pilfering these berries, said to me: 'Oh, Monsieur, what are you doing there? Don't you realize that those berries are poisonous?' 'Poisonous?', I cried, astonished. 'They certainly are', he replied, 'and everyone knows it so well that no locals ever think of trying them.' I looked at Monsieur Bovier and said to him: 'So why didn't you warn me?' 'Ah, Monsieur,' he replied, respectfully, 'I didn't dare take the liberty.' I started laughing at this Dauphiné humility,* while nevertheless ending my little meal. I was convinced, and still am, that no natural thing which tastes pleasant can be harmful to our bodies, unless we have excessive amounts of it. However, I must admit that I kept a close eye on myself the rest of the day, but I escaped with just a little worry; I ate very well that evening, slept better still, and got up the next morning in perfect health, having the previous day eaten fifteen or twenty berries of this terrible *hippophae*,* which is poisonous even in very small amounts, according to what everyone in Grenoble told me the next day. This adventure amused me so much that whenever I remember it, I laugh at lawyer Bovier's singular discretion.

All my botanical walks, the varied impressions made on me by the places where I have seen striking things, the ideas they have stirred in me, and the incidents that became connected to them have all left me with impressions which are renewed by the sight of the plants I collected in those very places. I shall never again see those beautiful landscapes, those forests, those lakes, those groves, those rocks or those mountains, the sight of which has always touched my heart; but now that I can no longer roam about those glorious places, all I have to do is open my herbarium and it quickly transports me there. The pieces of plants that I gathered there are enough to remind me of the whole magnificent spectacle. This herbarium is for me a diary of my botanical expeditions which makes me set off on them again with renewed delight and which produces the effect of an optical chamber, showing them again before my very eyes.

It is the chain of secondary ideas that attracts me to botany. It brings together and recalls to my imagination all the ideas which please it most. It constantly reminds me of the meadows, the waters, the woods, the solitude, above all the peace and the tranquillity one finds in the midst of all those things. It makes me forget the persecution of men, their hate, their scorn, their insults, and all their evil deeds with which they have repaid my tender and sincere attachment to them. It transports me to peaceful places amongst good and simple folk like those with whom I used to live. It reminds me of my youth and my innocent pleasures, it makes me enjoy them all over again, and very often it makes me happy, even in the midst of the most miserable fate ever endured by a mortal.

EIGHTH WALK

Meditating on the state of my soul through every stage of my life, I am extremely struck by the lack of direct relationship between the different forms my destiny has taken and the habitual feelings of well-being or despondency they have stirred in me. The various periods of short-lived prosperity have left me with almost no pleasant memories of the close and lasting way in which they affected me, and by contrast, in all the hardships of my life I constantly felt full of tender, touching, and delightful emotions which, as they poured a healing balm over my wounded heart, seemed to turn its pain into pleasure, and the memory of which comes back to me on its own, without that of the adversities I experienced at the same time. It seems to me that I enjoyed the pleasure of existence more fully, that I really lived more fully, when my feelings, concentrated, as it were, around my heart by my destiny, were not wasted on all the things prized by men, which are of such little value in themselves and which are all supposedly happy people are concerned with.

When everything was in order around me and I was happy with everything surrounding me and with the sphere in which I had to live, I filled it with my affections. My expansive soul spread to other things, and, constantly drawn away from myself by a thousand different tastes and by delightful attachments which constantly occupied my heart, in a sense I forgot myself: I was entirely given over to what was foreign to me and I felt, in the continual agitation of my heart, all the instability of human things. This stormy life gave me neither inward peace nor outward tranquillity. Apparently happy, I had not a single feeling which could withstand the test of thought and which I could really take pleasure in. I was never perfectly happy with others or with myself. The tumult of the world stunned me, solitude bored me, and I constantly needed to be on the move and felt at ease nowhere. Yet I was acclaimed, well regarded, well received, and warmly welcomed wherever I went. I had not a single enemy, nobody wishing me ill, and nobody envying me. Since people sought only to oblige me, I often had the pleasure of obliging many people myself, and with neither possessions nor a role, nor a patron, nor any great talents which were well developed or well known, I enjoyed the advantages attached to such things, and I saw nobody of any rank whatsoever whose fate seemed preferable to mine. So what did I need to make me happy? I do not know, but I do know that I was not happy.

What is missing today to make me the most unfortunate of mortals? Nothing of what men have done. And yet, even in this deplorable state I would not change my being or my destiny for those of the most fortunate amongst them, and I still prefer to be me in all my wretchedness than to be one of those people in all their prosperity. Reduced to my own self, it is true that I feed on my own substance, but it does not run out and I am self-sufficient, even though I ruminate, as it were, on nothing and my dried-up imagination and worn-out ideas no longer give my heart any sustenance. My soul, obscured and obstructed by my organs, sinks daily beneath the weight of these heavy masses and no longer has the strength it needs to soar as it once did beyond its old frame.

Adversity forces us to turn back in on ourselves, and it is perhaps this which makes it most unbearable for most men. For my part, since I only have mistakes to reproach myself for, I blame them on my weakness and console myself, for premeditated evil never came near my heart.

However, short of being in a complete daze, how can one for a moment contemplate my situation without seeing how horrible they have made it and without dying of pain and despair? By contrast, I, the most sensitive of beings, contemplate it and am unmoved by it; and without having to struggle or force myself, I look at myself almost with indifference in a situation the sight of which perhaps no other man could bear without being terrified.

How have I reached this point? For I was far removed from this peaceful frame of mind when I first came to suspect that there was a plot in which I had quite unwittingly been ensnared for a long time. This new discovery overwhelmed me. The infamy and treachery took me by surprise; what decent soul is prepared for sufferings of this kind? One would have to deserve them to be able to foresee them. I fell into all the traps that were dug beneath my feet. Indignation, fury, and madness took hold of me, I lost my mind, my head was in convulsions, and in the horrible darkness in which they have constantly kept me buried, I could see no glimmer of light to guide me nor any support or foothold to keep me upright and help me to resist the despair that was dragging me down.

How could one possibly live happily and quietly in this awful state? Yet I am still in it, indeed more deeply than ever before, and I have regained my calm and peace, and I am living happily and quietly, and I laugh at the incredible torments that my persecutors continually inflict upon themselves while I remain in peace, busy with flowers, stamens, and childish things, never giving them a moment's thought.

How did this change happen? Naturally, imperceptibly, and painlessly. The initial shock was dreadful. I, who felt I deserved love and respect, who believed myself to be honoured and cherished as I deserved to be, suddenly found myself transformed into an awful monster, the like of which has never been seen before. I watched as an entire generation rushed headlong into this strange opinion without explanation, doubt, or shame, and without my even being able to discover the cause of this strange reversal. I struggled violently and succeeded only in further ensnaring myself. I wanted to force my persecutors to explain themselves to me, but they did not wish to. Having tormented myself for a long time but in vain, I had to stop to draw breath. And yet I still hoped, telling myself: 'Such foolish blindness, such absurd prejudice could never win over the whole of the human race. There are men of good sense who do not share this madness; there are just souls who loathe deceit and traitors. Let us look; I shall perhaps find such a man in the end, and if I find one, they will be confounded.' I looked in vain; I did not find him. The plot against me is universal, complete, and irrevocable, and it is certain that I shall end my days in this awful exile without ever working out the mystery behind it.

It is in this deplorable state that, after suffering for so long, instead of the despair which was to be, it seemed, my ultimate lot,

I recovered my serenity, tranquillity, peace, and even my happiness, since every day of my life brings me the pleasure of remembering the previous day's happiness, and I desire nothing more for the next day.

Where does this difference come from? From one thing alone. It is that I have learned to bear the yoke of necessity without complaining. It is that I was trying hard to hold on to a thousand different things at once and that, all these things having escaped me one by one and my being left only with my own self, I have finally regained a settled position. Under pressure from all sides, I keep my balance because, no longer clinging to anything, I lean only on myself.

When I used to protest so vehemently against public opinion, I still used to bear its yoke without realizing it. People want to be respected by those whom they respect, and as long as I was able to judge men, or at least some men, favourably, the judgements they made about me could not be a matter of indifference to me. I saw that the judgements made by the public are often fair, but I did not see that this very fairness was the product of chance, that the principles on which men base their opinions are drawn solely from their passions or their prejudices which are created by their passions, and that even when they make sound judgements, these too are often born of an unsound principle, such as when they pretend to honour the merits of a man who has enjoyed some success, not out of a spirit of fairness but in order to give themselves an appearance of impartiality while at the same time happily slandering the same man for other reasons.

But when, after long and fruitless searching, I saw that they all, without exception, remained committed to the most unjust and absurd plot that a demon could ever have invented; when I saw that, where I was concerned, reason was banished from every mind and justice from every heart; when I saw a frenzied generation giving itself over entirely to the blind fury of its leaders directed against an unfortunate individual who never harmed anyone, never wished anyone any harm, and never rendered evil for evil; and when, after looking in vain for ten years for a man, I had finally to snuff out my lantern* and exclaim: 'There is none to be found', then I began to see that I was alone on the earth, and I realized that my contemporaries were, where I was concerned, nothing but mechanical beings who acted only on impulse and whose actions I could calculate only according to the laws of motion. Whatever intention or passion that I could have supposed them to have in their souls, these would never have explained their behaviour towards me in any way I could comprehend. Thus it was that their inner state of mind stopped being of significance to me. All I saw in them now was masses that were stirred into action in different ways and that were devoid of all morality where I was concerned.

In all the ills that befall us, we think more about the intention behind them than the effect of them. A tile that falls off a roof can hurt us more but it will not injure us as much as a stone thrown deliberately by a malevolent hand. The blow sometimes misses, but the intention never does. The physical pain is what one feels the least in the onslaughts of fate, and when unfortunate people do not know whom to blame for their misfortunes, they blame destiny, which they personify and to which they give eyes and a mind with which it deliberately torments them. In this way, a gambler, angered by his losses, flies into a fury, but he does not know against whom. He imagines a fate which is deliberately bent on tormenting him, and finding something on which to feed his anger, he becomes incensed and enraged against the enemy he has created for himself. The wise man, who sees in all the misfortunes that befall him only the blows of blind necessity, has none of this mad agitation: he cries out in pain, but without losing his temper or getting angry; he feels only the physical effects of the evil to which he has fallen prey, and however much the blows may injure his body, not one of them can reach his heart.

To have come this far is impressive, but it is not far enough if one stops there. It would be like having cut down the evil but left the root behind. For this root is not in beings who are outside us; it is in ourselves, and it is from there that we have to work hard to pull it out completely. This is what I concluded as soon as I began coming to my senses. Since my reason revealed to me only absurdities in all the explanations I tried to give for what happened to me, I realized that the causes, instruments, and means of it all, which were unknown and inexplicable to me, should be of no significance to me whatsoever; that I should consider all the details of my destiny as the workings of simple fate in which I should presuppose no direction, intention, or moral cause; that I had to submit to it without arguing or resisting because to do that would be pointless; and that, since all that remained for me to do on earth was to consider myself a purely passive being, I should not waste on futile resistance to my destiny what strength I had left to withstand it. This is what I told myself; my reason and my heart acquiesced, but nevertheless I could feel that my heart was still grumbling. Where did this dissatisfaction come from? I looked for and found the answer: it came from my self-love which, having become indignant with men, now rebelled against reason.

This discovery was not as easy to make as one might imagine, since a persecuted, innocent man too often interprets his petty, individual pride as a pure love of justice. But equally, once the real source has been identified, it is easy to stem or at least divert. Self-esteem is the strongest motive felt by proud souls; self-love, which breeds illusions, disguises itself, and passes itself off as this self-esteem, but when the fraud is finally exposed and self-love can no longer hide itself, from that point on it is no longer to be feared, and although one may struggle to destroy it, one can at least overcome it with ease.

I was never greatly given to self-love, but this artificial passion had come to appear more noble to me when I was in the world, and above all when I became an author; I perhaps had less of it than other authors, but I still had an enormous amount. The terrible lessons I received soon cut it down to its original size: to begin with it rebelled against injustice, but in the end it treated it with disdain. Turning back in on my soul and severing the links with the outside which make it so demanding, and rejecting all comparisons and preferences, it was content for me to be good on my own terms; and so, as it became love of myself again, it returned to the natural order and freed me from the yoke of public opinion.*

From then on my soul was at peace again and I was almost perfectly happy. Whatever situation we may find ourselves in, it is only self-love that makes us constantly unhappy. When it falls silent and reason speaks, this consoles us at last for all the ills which we have been unable to avoid. It even destroys them, in so far as they do not affect us immediately, since the best way of avoiding their sharpest attacks is to stop paying attention to them. These ills are as nothing to the person who does not think about them. Insults, reprisals, wrongs, outrages, and injustices are as nothing to the person who only sees in the hardships he suffers the hardship itself and not the intention behind it and whose place in his own self-esteem does not depend on the esteem that others may choose to show him. However men wish to see me, they cannot change my being, and in spite of their power and all their secret plots, I shall continue, whatever they may do, to be what I am in spite of them. It is true that their attitudes towards me have an influence on my actual situation: the barrier that they have placed between them and me denies me every source of subsistence and assistance in my old age and in my need. It even makes money useless to me, because it cannot buy me the help I need: there is no longer any exchange, mutual aid, or correspondence between them and me. Alone in the midst of them, I have only myself to turn to, and I am very weak at my age and in my situation. These misfortunes are great, but they have lost all their strength for me now that I know how to endure them without getting angry. The times when I feel real need are still rare. Foresight and imagination multiply their number, and it is these ongoing feelings that make us anxious and unhappy.* It means nothing to me, knowing that I shall suffer tomorrow: all I need to be at peace is not to suffer today. I am not affected by the ills I foresee, but only by those I actually feel, and this reduces them to very little. Alone, sick, and abandoned in my bed, I could die of poverty, cold, and hunger there without anyone caring. But what does it matter if I myself do not care and am no more affected than anyone else by my destiny, whatever it may be? Is it not something, above all at my age, to have learned to regard life and death, sickness and health, wealth and poverty, and fame and slander with equal indifference? All other old people worry about everything; I worry about nothing: whatever may happen, it is all a matter of indifference to me, and this indifference is not the fruit of my wisdom, but of my enemies.

Let us learn, then, to treat these advantages as compensation for the suffering they inflict upon me. In making me impervious to adversity, they have done me more good than they would have done, had they spared me its attacks. If I had not experienced it, I might still fear it now, whereas by overcoming it, I no longer fear it.

In the midst of my life's afflictions, this attitude allows me to indulge my natural insouciance almost as much as if I were living in the greatest prosperity. Apart from the brief moments when I am reminded by the things around me of my most painful anxieties, the rest of the time, following my inclinations and indulging the affections which attract me, my heart still feeds on the feelings for which it was created, and I enjoy them with imaginary beings who produce them and share them with me, as if these beings really existed. They exist for me, since I created them, and I do not worry about their betraying or abandoning me. They will last as long as my misfortunes themselves and will suffice to make me forget them.

Everything brings me back to the happy and sweet life for which I was born. I spend three quarters of my life either busy with instructive and even pleasant things, to which I am delighted to devote my mind and my senses, or with the children of my imagination, which I created according to my heart's desires, whose feelings are nourished by contact with them, or else with myself, contented with myself and already full of the happiness I feel is owing to me. In all this, only love of myself is at work, and self-love has nothing to do with it. The same cannot be said of those sad moments I still spend among men, the plaything of their treacherous affections, their overblown and derisive compliments, and their honeyed malice. However I get caught, self-love always plays a role. The hatred and animosity I see in their hearts through their crude disguises fill my heart with pain, and the idea of so naively being duped compounds this pain with a very childish irritation, the product of a foolish self-love which I know full well is stupid but which I cannot control. The efforts I have made to become inured to these insulting and mocking looks are incredible. A hundred times I have walked along the avenues and in the most public of places with the sole aim of learning to put up with these cruel lies; not only was I unable to do so, I did not even make any progress, and all my painful yet fruitless efforts left me just as susceptible as before to being upset, hurt, or angered.

Dominated, whether I like it or not, by my senses, I have never been able to resist the impressions they make on me, and as long as an object affects them, my heart does not fail to be affected too; but these passing affections last only as long as the sensation that causes them. The presence of a hateful man affects me violently, but as soon as he has gone, the feelings stop; as soon as I no longer see him, I stop thinking about him. It does nothing to me to know that he is going to concern himself with me, for I am unable to concern myself with him. The suffering which I do not actually feel has not the slightest effect on me; the persecutor whom I do not see is as nothing for me. I realize this gives an advantage to those who control my destiny. So let them control it as they wish. I would prefer them to torment me unhindered than to be forced to think about them in order to protect myself from their blows.

The way my senses affect my heart is the one torment in my life. On the days when I see nobody, I no longer think about my destiny, I am no longer conscious of it, I no longer suffer, and I am happy and contented, with neither distraction nor obstacle in my way. But I rarely escape any physical assault, and when I am least thinking about it, a gesture, a sinister look that I catch sight of, a poisoned remark that I hear or a malicious person I meet is enough to upset me. All I can do in such circumstances is to forget as quickly as possible and run away. My heart's distress disappears with the object that caused it, and I become calm again as soon as I am alone. Or if anything continues to worry me, it is the fear of chancing upon some other cause of pain. That is my only worry, but it is enough to spoil my happiness. I live in the middle of Paris. When I leave home, I long for the countryside and solitude, but they are to be found so far away that before I can breathe easily, I come across a thousand things that oppress my heart, and half of the day is spent in anguish before I have reached the refuge I was looking for. I am fortunate, though, when I am left to make my way in peace. The moment when I escape the train of the malevolent is one to be savoured, and as soon as I am under the trees and surrounded by greenery, it is as if I were in the earthly paradise, and I experience an inner pleasure as intense as if I were the happiest of mortals.

I remember perfectly how, in my brief periods of prosperity, these same solitary walks which today I find so sweet I then found insipid and tedious. When I was staying with someone in the country, the need for exercise and fresh air often made me go out alone, and, escaping like a thief, I would go walking in the park or in the countryside, but, far from finding the happy calm that I enjoy there today, I carried with me the agitation of futile ideas which had occupied me in the salon; the memory of the company I had left behind followed me in my solitude; the mists of self-love and the tumult of the world soured the freshness of the groves in my eyes and troubled my secluded peace. I had fled in vain to the depths of the woods: an importunate crowd followed me everywhere and veiled the whole of nature from me. It is only once I had cut myself off from social passions and their dismal retinue that I rediscovered nature and all her charms.

Convinced that it is impossible to repress these first, involuntary instincts, I have given up trying. Whenever I am under attack, I allow my blood to boil and anger and indignation to take hold of my senses; I grant nature this initial explosion which all my strength could neither stop nor hinder. I try simply to prevent it having any consequences before it has the chance to do so. My eyes flash, my face is aflame, my limbs tremble, and I have suffocating palpitations: these are purely physical reactions and reasoning can do nothing about them; but having let nature have this initial explosion, one can become one's own master again as one gradually regains one's senses; this is what for a long time I tried in vain to do, but in the end I have had more success. And instead of using my strength to resist in vain, I wait for the moment of victory by letting my reason have its way, since it only speaks when it can make itself heard. Ah! Alas, what am I saying? My reason? It would be quite wrong of me to attribute this victory to my reason, for it has very little to do with it. Everything comes equally from a changeable temperament that is stirred up by an impetuous wind but which calms down again as soon as the wind stops blowing. It is my ardent nature which stirs me up, and my nonchalant nature which calms me down. I give way to whatever impulses I happen to feel: every shock provokes a rapid and short-lived reaction in me; as soon as the shock is over, the reaction ceases: nothing I am made to feel can last for long in me. All the ups and downs of fate and all men's machinations have little hold over a man like me. In order for any suffering to last, the cause would have to be constantly renewed. For any pause, no matter how brief, is enough for me to regain composure. I am at men's mercy as long as they can have an effect on my senses; but at the first moment of respite, I return to being what nature intended: whatever may happen, that is my most constant state and the one through which, in spite of destiny, I enjoy a kind of happiness for which I feel I was made. I have described this state in one of my reveries.* It suits me so well that I desire nothing other than for it to last, and my only fear is seeing it disturbed. The evil that men have done me in no way affects me; only the fear of the evil that they might yet do me is capable of unsettling me; but being certain that they have no new hold over me by which they could affect me for ever, I laugh at all their ploys and enjoy being me in spite of them.

NINTH WALK

HAPPINESS is a lasting state which does not seem to be made for man in this world. Everything on earth is in a continual flux which allows nothing to take a constant form. Everything changes around us. We ourselves change, and nobody can be sure of loving tomorrow what he loves today. For this reason, all our plans for perfect happiness in this life are idle dreams. Let us make the most of mental contentment when it comes to us; let us be careful not to be responsible for driving it away, but let us not make plans to tie it down either, because such plans are sheer folly. I have seen few if any happy men; but I have often seen contented hearts, and of all the things that have struck me, this is the one that has made me most contented too. I believe this is a natural consequence of the power that sensations have on my inner feelings. Happiness has no external sign: to recognize it, one would need to be able to read in the happy man's heart; but contentment can be seen in the eyes, the bearing, the voice, and the walk, and it seems to communicate itself to the person who sees it. Is there any sweeter delight than seeing a whole people filled with joy on a feast day and all their hearts open up to the expansive rays of pleasure, which passes quickly but intensely through the clouds of life?

Three days ago, Monsieur P.* came to see me, extraordinarily eager to show me Monsieur d'Alembert's eulogy of Madame Geoffrin.* Before reading it, he laughed long and hard at all the work's ridiculous neologisms and at the witty puns with which he said it was filled. As he started reading, he was still laughing; I listened to him solemnly, which made him calm down, and when he realized that I was not following his example, he finally stopped laughing. The longest and most mannered part of the text dealt with the pleasure Madame Geoffrin took in seeing children and making them talk. The author rightly saw in this attitude proof of her good character. But he did not stop there, and unhesitatingly accused those who did not share her taste of having a bad character and being wicked, going so far as to state that if one were to question those being sent to the gallows or the wheel about this, they would all admit that they had not loved children. These assertions created an odd effect in the middle of such a text. Even if they were all true, was this the right occasion to make them, and did the eulogy of a respectable woman need to be sullied with images of punishment and crime? I quickly realized what the motive was behind this unpleasant sham, and when Monsieur P. had finished reading, I said what I thought was good in the eulogy and added that the author had not so much friendship as hatred in his heart when he wrote it.

The following day, since the weather was quite fine, although cold, I set out on a walk to the Military Academy,* expecting to find some mosses there in full flower. As I walked, I reflected on the visit I had received the previous day and on Monsieur d'Alembert's text, into which I was sure the unnecessary passage had not been inserted unintentionally, and the deliberate way in which this pamphlet was brought to me of all people, from whom everything is normally hidden, was enough to show me quite clearly what its real purpose was. I had put my children in the Foundlings' Hospital,* and for this alone I was misrepresented as an unnatural father, and so, developing and entertaining this idea, people had gradually drawn the obvious conclusion that I hated children; as I followed this chain of thought step by step, I came to admire the artful way in which human ingenuity can turn white into black. For I do not believe that any man has ever loved seeing little children romping and playing together more than I do, and I often stop in the street and in the avenues to watch their naughty tricks and little games with an interest which I cannot see anyone else sharing. The very day that Monsieur P. came to see me, I had had a visit an hour earlier from the two little Du Soussoi children, my landlord's youngest, the elder of whom must be seven. They had come to embrace me so eagerly and I had returned their caresses so tenderly that, in spite of the difference in age, they had seemed truly to enjoy being with me, and for my part I was overjoyed to see that my old face had not repelled them; indeed, the younger boy seemed to come back to me so willingly that, more childlike than they, I soon felt particularly attached to him, and I was as sorry to see him leave as if he had been one of my own.

I can see that the reproach of my having put my children in the Foundlings' Hospital has easily degenerated, with a little distortion, into that of being an unnatural father and a child-hater. However, it is certain that what influenced me most in taking this decision was my fear that their fate would almost inevitably be, under any other circumstances, a thousand times worse.* If I had been more indifferent about what would happen to them and unable to bring them up myself, I would in my position have had to let them be brought up by their mother, who would have spoiled them, and her family, who would have turned them into monsters. What Mahomet did to Séide* is as nothing compared to what would have been done to them with regard to me, and the traps subsequently laid for me about this are enough to convince me that the plot had been hatched. In truth, I was at that point far from foreseeing these dreadful schemes, but I knew that the least dangerous education for them was that offered by the Foundlings' Hospital, and so I put them there. I would do it again, and with much less hesitation, if I had to, and I am sure that no father is more affectionate than I would have been towards them, once habit had combined with nature.

If I have made some progress in knowing the human heart, it is because of the pleasure I took in seeing and observing children. In my youth this same pleasure was a kind of obstacle to me, since I played so happily and enthusiastically with children that I hardly thought to study them. But when, as I grew older, I saw that my aged face unnerved them, I stopped bothering them and preferred to deprive myself of a pleasure rather than disturb their happiness; satisfied thereafter with making do with watching their games and all their little ways, I found compensation for my sacrifice in the knowledge which these observations equipped me with about the first and true impulses of nature, about which all our scholars know nothing. I set out in my writings the proof that I had engaged in this research too carefully not to have enjoyed doing so, and it would surely be the most incredible thing in the world if *Héloïse* and *Émile* were the work of a man who did not love children.

I never had presence of mind or ease of speech, but since my misfortunes began, my tongue and my head have become increasingly prone to confusion. Both ideas and the words I need to express them escape me, and nothing demands better judgement and a more careful choice of words than talking to children. What makes this confusion worse still for me is the presence of people listening attentively to me and the interpretations they give and the importance they attach to every word that comes from a man who, having written specifically for children, is supposed to utter nothing but oracles when speaking to them. This extreme awkwardness and my sense of incompetence trouble and disconcert me, and I would be much more at ease in front of a monarch from Asia than in front of a little child whom I have to make chat with me.

Another problem now keeps me even further away from them, and since my misfortunes began, while I still enjoy seeing them, I am no longer on such familiar terms with them. Children do not like old age: they find the appearance of decrepit nature hideous, the repugnance I see them feeling hurts me deeply, and I prefer to refrain from caressing them rather than embarrass or disgust them. This reluctance, which only affects truly loving souls, is as nothing for all our learned gentlemen and ladies. Madame Geoffrin cared very little about whether or not children enjoyed being with her as long as she enjoyed being with them. But for me this pleasure is worse than non-existent: it is negative when it is not reciprocated, and I am no longer in a position or of an age to see a child's little heart bursting forth together with mine. If that could happen to me again, the pleasure I would feel would be all the more intense for having become so rare, and indeed this is what I felt the other morning when I had the pleasure of an affectionate exchange with the little Du Soussoi children, not only because the maid who brought them to see me did not greatly intimidate me and I felt less of a need to weigh my words in front of her, but also because their cheerful looks when they approached me remained with them throughout and they did not appear to become unhappy or weary of being with me.

Oh, if I could still enjoy a few moments of pure, heartfelt affection, even if only from a babe in arms, if I could still see in people's eyes the joy and satisfaction of being with me, how these brief but sweet effusions of my heart would compensate me for so many woes and afflictions. Ah, I would no longer be obliged to seek among animals the kind looks that I am now refused by human beings. I can judge on the basis of examples which are very few in number but which are always dear to my memory. Here is one which, in any other circumstances, I would have almost entirely forgotten and which made an impression on me that clearly shows just what a miserable state I was in. Two years ago, having gone for a walk over towards Nouvelle France,* I continued past it and then, going off to the left and intending to skirt around Montmartre, I passed through the village of Clignancourt.* I was walking along distractedly and dreamily without looking about me when suddenly I felt someone grab me around the knees. I looked down and saw a little child of five or six, hugging my knees with all his might and looking at me with such a friendly and affectionate air that I was stirred to the depths of my soul and said to myself: 'This is how I would have been treated by my own children.' I picked the child up in my arms, kissed him several times in a kind of rapture, and then continued on my way. As I walked, I felt that I was missing something, that a nascent need was calling me to retrace my steps. I blamed myself for having left the child so suddenly, and I thought I saw in his apparently spontaneous act a sort of inspiration that I ought not to scorn. In the end, giving in to temptation, I turned back, ran up to the child, embraced him again, gave him some money to buy some Nanterre cakes* from the seller who happened to be passing by, and started making him chatter. I asked him where his father was; he pointed to a man hooping barrels. I was about to leave the child in order to go and speak to him when I realized that an unpleasant-looking man had got there before me who seemed to me to be one of those spies who are constantly following me. While this man was whispering something to him, I saw the cooper start staring at me with a look that was in no way friendly. This sight immediately made my heart grow heavy and I left the father and child even more speedily than I had returned, but in a less agreeable agitation, which completely changed my attitude.

Since then, however, I have quite often felt the same way again: I have several times passed through Clignancourt in the hope of seeing the child again, but I have seen neither him nor his father, and all I have left of that meeting is a quite vivid memory forever tinged with affection and sadness, like all the emotions which still occasionally touch my heart and which a painful reaction always puts an end to by closing my heart in on itself again.

There are compensations for everything. If my pleasures are rare and short-lived, I also enjoy them more intensely when they do come than I would if I were more used to them; I ruminate on them, as it were, as I often think about them, and although they are rare, if they were pure and untainted, I would perhaps be happier than I was when I was prosperous. In extreme poverty, a little makes one rich. A beggar who finds an *écu** is more moved than a rich man would be who found a purse full of gold. People would laugh if they could see the impression made on my soul by the slightest pleasures of this kind, which I can conceal from the watchful eye of my persecutors. One of the most recent of these was four or five years ago, and whenever I recall it, I feel overjoyed to have made such good use of it.

One Sunday my wife and I had gone to have lunch at the Porte Maillot.* After lunch we walked through the Bois de Boulogne as far as La Muette,* where we sat down on the grass in the shade, waiting for the sun to go down before heading gently home by way of Passy.* A group of about twenty little girls, led by a kind of nun, came along, and some sat down, others played about quite close to us. While they were playing, a wafer-seller passed by with his drum and wheel, looking for customers.* I could see that the little girls were longing to have some wafers, and two or three of them, who apparently had a few *liards*,* asked if they could play. While their governess was hesitating and arguing with them, I called the wafer-seller over and said to him: 'Let all these young ladies take it in turns to draw tickets, and I shall pay for them all.' These words filled the whole company with a joy which would have been worth all the money in my purse, had I spent it all in this way.

Seeing that they were rushing up in a rather confused way, with their governess's permission I made them all stand to one side and then go over to the other side one by one as they drew their tickets. Although there were no blanks and there would be at least one wafer for each girl with nothing, so that none of them could be really upset, in order to make the festivities jollier still, I secretly told the wafer-seller to put his usual skill to unusual ends by making as many good numbers come up as he could possibly manage and that I would reward him for doing so. Thanks to this foresight, almost a hundred wafers were given out, although each young girl drew only one ticket each, as I was unwavering on this, not wanting to encourage any abuses or show any favouritism which might have led to some girls being upset. My wife subtly persuaded those who had plenty of wafers to share them with their friends, and in so doing almost everyone received the same number and the joy was spread more evenly around the group.

I asked the nun if she would like to take her turn in drawing a ticket, though I was very afraid that she would disdainfully reject my offer; she accepted it with good grace, drew a ticket as her charges had, and took what was hers unaffectedly: I was infinitely grateful to her, and I found in her behaviour a sort of politeness which I liked very much and which is, I believe, worth any amount of affected politeness. Throughout this whole process there were disputes which were brought before my judgement seat, and seeing these little girls coming one after another to plead their cause, I noticed that, although none of them was pretty, some of them were so charming that one forgot their ugliness.

We eventually parted company, very pleased with each other; and that afternoon was one of those from throughout my life that I remember with the greatest satisfaction. The festivities were, moreover, not expensive, but for the thirty *sols** at most that I spent, there was more than a thousand *écus*' worth of happiness, since true pleasure is not measured by what it costs, and joy goes better with *liards* than with *louis.** I have on several other occasions returned to the same place at the same time, hoping to meet the little band there again, but to no avail.

This reminds me of another amusement of much the same kind, the memory of which has been with me for a much longer time. It was during that unhappy period when, mixing with the rich and with men of letters, I was sometimes reduced to sharing in their sorry pleasures. I was at La Chevrette* at the time of the name-day of the master of the house; his whole family had gathered there to celebrate it, and to this end the whole array of noisy pleasures was deployed. Games, theatricals, banquets, fireworks: nothing was spared. There was no time to draw breath, and instead of enjoying ourselves, we were left stunned. After the dinner we went out for some air in the avenue; a kind of fair was being held there. There was dancing; the gentlemen deigned to dance with the peasant girls, but the ladies kept their dignity. Gingerbread was being sold there. A young man in the company took it upon himself to buy some to throw piece by piece into the crowd, and they took so much pleasure in seeing all these peasants rushing, fighting, and pushing each other over to get at it that everybody wanted to join in the fun. So gingerbread flew in all directions, and girls and boys ran about, piled on top of one another, and broke arms and legs: everybody thought this was charming. I did the same as all the rest because I felt awkward, although deep down I was not enjoying myself as much as they were. But I soon tired of emptying my purse in order to have people crushed, so I left the good company and went walking alone through the fair. The variety of things to be seen amused me for a long time. Amongst others I saw five or six chimneysweeps gathered around a little girl who still had a dozen pathetic little apples on her stall that she would have been only too happy to be rid of. The chimneysweeps for their part would have been only too happy to relieve her of them, but they only had two or three *liards* between them, which was not enough to make great inroads into the apples. For them, this stall was the Garden of the Hesperides, and the little girl the dragon guarding it.* This comic scene amused me for a long time; I finally brought it to its climax by buying the apples from the little girl and making her share them out amongst the little boys. Then I had one of the sweetest sights that can delight a man's heart, that of seeing joy combined with innocence of youth spreading all around me, for the onlookers also shared in it as they watched, and I, partaking of this joy at such little cost to myself, had the additional joy of feeling that I had created it.

As I compared this entertainment with those I had just left behind, I had the satisfaction of feeling the difference that separates healthy tastes and natural pleasures from those that are born of opulence and are little more than mocking pleasures and exclusive tastes created by disdain. For what sort of pleasure could one possibly take in seeing herds of men, degraded by poverty, piling on top of each other, suffocating and brutally crushing one another in a desperate attempt to grab a few pieces of gingerbread which had been trampled underfoot and covered in mud?

For my part, when I have reflected on the sort of pleasure I enjoyed on such occasions, I have found that it consisted less in a feeling of doing good than in seeing contented faces. This sight has a charm for me which, although it touches my heart, seems to come uniquely from my sensations. If I could not see the satisfaction that I cause, even if I were convinced of it, I would enjoy it only half as much. Indeed, for me it is a disinterested pleasure which is not dependent on the role I may play in it. For in popular celebrations I have always been very attracted by the pleasure of seeing happy faces. However, this expectation has often been frustrated in France, a nation which claims to be so cheerful but which shows so little of this cheerfulness when at play. In the past I often used to go to cabarets to see the lower classes dancing, but their dances were so poorly done and their bearing so pitiful and clumsy that I would leave more saddened than gladdened. But in Geneva and Switzerland, where laughter is not continually wasted on ridiculous dirty tricks, everything in festivities exudes contentment and cheerfulness, poverty does not rear its ugly head, nor does pomp parade its insolence; well-being, fraternity, and concord incline hearts to open up, and often in the transports of innocent joy, complete strangers accost one another, embrace, and invite one another to join together in enjoying the day's pleasures.* In order to enjoy these delightful festivities myself, I do not need to be taking part in them; it is enough for me to see them: by seeing them, I share in them, and amongst all these happy faces, I am convinced that there is no heart happier than mine.

Although this is only a pleasure born of sensation, it nevertheless has a moral cause, and the proof of this is that the same sight, instead of delighting and pleasing me, can fill me with pain and indignation when I know that the signs of pleasure and joy on the faces of the wicked are nothing but signs that their wickedness has been satisfied. Only the signs of innocent joy delight my heart. Those of cruel and mocking joy wound and distress it, even if it has nothing to do with me. No doubt these signs cannot be exactly the same, since they are based on such different principles: but nevertheless they are all signs of joy, and the visible differences between them are certainly not proportionate to the differences between the emotions they arouse in me.

The signs of pain and suffering affect me still more, so much so that I find it impossible to bear them without myself being stirred by emotions which are perhaps yet more intense than those which they express. My imagination reinforces sensation and makes me identify myself with the suffering being and often causes me more anguish than he himself feels. A discontented face is another sight that it is impossible for me to bear, especially if I suspect that this discontent concerns me. I cannot say how many *écus* were extracted from me by the grumpy and gloomy faces of valets serving unwillingly in the houses to which I used to be foolish enough to let myself be dragged and where the servants always made me pay a very high price for their masters' hospitality.* Always affected too much by things I see, and particularly by signs of pleasure or suffering, affection or dislike, I let myself be carried away by these external impressions without ever being able to avoid them other than by fleeing. A sign, a gesture or a glance from a stranger is enough to disturb my peace or calm my suffering: I am only my own master when I am alone; at all other times I am the plaything of all those around me.

I used to enjoy living in society, when I saw only affection in everyone's eyes or at worst indifference in the eyes of those to whom I was unknown. But today, when as much care is taken to show my face to people as to hide my true character from them, I cannot set foot in the street without finding myself surrounded by distressing things; I quickly hurry off to the countryside; as soon as I see the greenery, I begin to breathe. Is it any surprise that I love solitude? I see only animosity on men's faces, and nature always smiles at me.

However, I must admit that I still feel pleasure in living among men as long as my face is unknown to them. But this is a pleasure which I am rarely allowed to enjoy. A few years ago I still liked walking through villages and, in the mornings, seeing workers repairing their flails or women in their doorways with their children. There was something about this sight that touched my heart. I sometimes stopped, unthinkingly, to watch the little ways of these fine folk, and I felt myself sighing without knowing why. I do not know if it was noticed that I was touched by this little pleasure and there was therefore a desire to rob me of it, but the change I saw on people's faces as I walked past and the way they looked at me made me realize that someone had taken great care to remove my incognito. The same thing happened to me, and in a yet more striking fashion, at the Invalides.* I have always been interested in this fine establishment. I can never look without emotion and veneration at those groups of good old men who can say like those of Lacedaemon:

> We were, in former days,
> Young, valiant, and brave.*

One of my favourite walks was around the Military Academy, and I used to enjoy meeting here and there some of the veterans who, retaining their old military courtesy, saluted me as I went by. This salute, which my heart returned to them a hundred-fold, delighted me and heightened my pleasure at seeing them. Since I am unable to conceal anything of what moves me, I often talked about the veterans and about how seeing them affected me. That is all it took. Some time later, I noticed that I was no longer a stranger to them, or rather that I was much more of a stranger to them than I had been, since they now looked at me in the same way as the general public did. No more courtesy, no more greetings. An off-putting manner and an unwelcoming look had taken the place of their original politeness. The sincerity of their former profession did not allow them, as others do, to disguise their animosity under a sneering and treacherous mask; they displayed quite openly the most violent hatred towards me, and so extreme is my wretched state that I am forced to respect most of all those who disguise their fury the least.

Since that time, I have taken less pleasure in walking over by the Invalides; however, since my feelings for them are not dependent on theirs for me, I cannot look at these former defenders of their country with anything but respect and affection: but I find it very hard to find myself so poorly repaid by them for the justice I do them. When I happen to meet one of them who has escaped the general instruction or who, not knowing my face, shows no aversion to me, the courteous greeting I receive from him is enough to make up for the rudeness of all the others. I forget them and think only about him, and I imagine that he has a soul like mine, which hatred can never reach. I had this very pleasure last year when I was crossing the river to go walking on the Île des Cygnes.* A poor old veteran in a boat was waiting for people to cross with him. I stepped into the boat and told the boatman to set off. The current was strong and the crossing was long. I hardly dared speak to the veteran for fear of being spoken to rudely and rebuffed as usual, but his courteous appearance reassured me. We chatted. He seemed to me to be a man of good sense and good morals. I was surprised and charmed by his open and affable manner, I was not used to such kindness; my surprise ceased when I learned that he had just arrived from the provinces. I realized that he had not yet been shown my face or given his instructions. I took advantage of my incognito to have a few moments of conversation with a man, and the delight I found in doing so made me aware of how the value of the most common of pleasures can be increased by their being rare. As he got out of the boat, he prepared to hand over his two poor *liards*. I paid for the crossing and begged him to put his money away, trembling lest he take offence. That did not happen; on the contrary, he seemed moved by my thoughtfulness in paying and above all in helping him, because he was older than me, to get out of the boat. Who would have thought that I was childlike enough to cry with pleasure? I was dying to hand him a 24 *sols* coin so that he could get some tobacco, but I never dared. The same embarrassment which held me back then has often prevented me since from doing good deeds which would have filled me with joy, and abstaining from them has only made me regret my weakness. On this occasion, having left my old veteran, I soon consoled myself with the thought that I would have, as it were, contradicted my own principles if I had placed on courteous actions the sort of monetary value that degrades their nobility and tarnishes their disinterestedness. One should hasten to help those in need, but in everyday human dealings, let us allow natural good will and politeness each to do its work without ever letting anything venal or mercantile dare come close to such a pure source and corrupt or sully it. It is said that in Holland people expect to be paid for telling you the time or showing you the way. It must be a very contemptible people that can trade in the simplest duties of humanity in this way.

I have noticed that only in Europe is hospitality bought and sold. Throughout Asia you are lodged for free. I realize that it is not so easy to find your creature comforts there. But is it not something to be able to say to yourself: 'I am a man and am taken in as a guest by humans. It is pure humanity that gives me shelter'? Minor hardships are easy to endure when the heart is better treated than the body.

TENTH WALK

TODAY, Palm Sunday,* it is exactly fifty years since I first met Madame de Warens.* She was twenty-eight then, having been born with the century.* I was not yet seventeen,* and my nascent temperament, which I was still unaware of, made my naturally ardent heart burn with renewed heat. If it was unsurprising that she should develop an affection for a lively but gentle, modest, and quite pleasant-looking young man, it was even less surprising that a charming, intelligent, and graceful woman should make me feel not only gratitude but also more tender feelings which I was unable to distinguish from it. But what is more unusual is that this one moment determined my whole life and produced, through an inevitable logic, the destiny of the rest of my days.* My soul, whose most precious faculties had not yet been fully developed by my bodily organs, still had no definite form. It was waiting somehow impatiently for the moment that would give it form, but this moment, though hastened by this meeting, did not come for a good while, and with my simple ways, given to me by my education, I saw this delightful but short-lived state stretching out far ahead of me, where love and innocence inhabit the same heart together. She had sent me away.* Everything called me back to her, I had to return. This return decided my destiny, and a long time before I possessed her, I lived solely in her and for her. Ah, if only I had satisfied her heart in the way she satisfied mine. What peaceful and delightful days we would have spent together. We did have some such days, but how brief and fleeting they were, and what a fate followed them. Not a day goes by without my remembering with joy and emotion that one, short time in my life when I was fully myself, unadulterated and unhindered, and when I can really say that I lived. I can say more or less the same as the Praetorian Prefect who, having been disgraced under Vespasian, went off to the country to end his days in peace: 'I have spent seventy years on earth and have lived for seven of them.'* Had it not been for this short but precious period, I would perhaps have remained uncertain about myself, for throughout the rest of my life, weak and unresisting, I have been so shaken, tossed, and pulled about by others' passions that, almost passive in such a stormy life, I would struggle to identify what there is of mine in my own conduct, so unceasingly has harsh necessity weighed down upon me. But during those few years, loved by a very gentle and obliging woman, I did what I wanted to do, I was what I wanted to be, and, through the use I made of my leisure time, helped by her teaching and example, I was able to give my still simple and naïve soul the form which was better suited to it and which it has retained ever since. The taste for solitude and contemplation was born in my heart together with the expansive and tender feelings whose purpose it is to feed it. Turmoil and noise constrain and suffocate them, calm and peace revive and intensify them. I need to retire within myself in order to love. I persuaded Mama* to live in the country. An isolated house on a valley slope was our refuge,* and it is there that, in the space of four or five years, I enjoyed a century of life and a pure, complete happiness, the delights of which outweigh all that is dreadful in my current fate. I needed a female friend after my own heart, and I had her. I had longed for the countryside, and I had obtained it; I could not bear subjection, and I was perfectly free, indeed better than free because, subject only to my own affections, I only did what I wanted to do. All my time was filled with loving cares and country pursuits. I wanted nothing other than for this sweet state to continue. The only thing distressing me was the fear that it would not continue for long, and this fear, born of the difficulties of our situation, was not unfounded. From then on I sought to ensure I had both distractions from this anxiety and the means by which to avoid its coming true. I decided that a treasure trove of talents was the surest protection against poverty, and I resolved to use my free time to ensure I was able, if possible, one day to repay the best of women for all the help I had received from her.

EXPLANATORY NOTES

3 *for fifteen years or more*: since Rousseau began writing his *Reveries* in September 1776, he may be alluding here to his flight from Montmorency in June 1762 following the publication of *Émile*, which was condemned by the Parlement de Paris, who also ordered the author's arrest.

4 *a frenzy which has taken no less than ten years to subside*: in spring 1767, some nine and a half years before beginning the *Reveries*, Rousseau thought that David Hume had drawn him into a trap in England, and fled in May that year.

5 *irrevocably fixed for evermore*: it is impossible to say with any certainty what this event was, though it could be the death of his sometime protector, the prince de Conti, on 2 August 1776, about a month before Rousseau started writing the *Reveries*.

6 *trying to ensure that they survive for posterity*: an allusion to *Rousseau Judge of Jean-Jacques: Dialogues* (*Rousseau juge de Jean-Jacques: Dialogues*), a work of self-defence, made up of three dialogues, which Rousseau wrote between 1772 and 1776. Having failed in his attempt to place the manuscript of his work on the high altar of Notre-Dame, Paris, on 24 February 1776, he tried to ensure its posterity by giving a copy to Condillac as well as a copy of the first dialogue to the young Englishman Brooke Boothby, who published it in Lichfield in 1780; in 1778 he gave the complete manuscript to his friend Paul Moultou, who helped to have it published in 1782.

the doctors: in Book 8 of the *Confessions*, Rousseau describes how he lost faith in doctors: 'For several years now, tortured by urinary retention, I had been entirely in the hands of the doctors, who, without alleviating my pain, had exhausted my strength and destroyed my constitution. . . . Resolving, whether I was cured or killed, to dispense with doctors and with medicines, I said farewell to them for ever and began to live from day to day' (trans. Angela Scholar, ed. Patrick Coleman (Oxford: Oxford University Press, 2000), 380).

the Oratorians: a secular congregation of priests living in community without vows; the French Oratory was founded in 1611 by Pierre de Bérulle. Rousseau had enjoyed a close relationship with the Oratorians at Montmorency, namely père Alamanni and père Mandard, to whom he refers in Book 11 of the *Confessions* (p. 567), but they fell out over *Émile*; and when the former priest of Montmorency, père de Muly, was appointed head of the Oratory in 1773, Rousseau thought that the whole organization had turned against him.

7 *my Confessions*: on the relationship between Rousseau's *Reveries* and his *Confessions*, see the Introduction, above, p. xiii.

7 *I shall soon have to render*: this echoes the beginning of the *Confessions*: 'Let the trumpet of judgement sound when it will, I will present myself with this book in my hand before the Supreme Judge' (p. 5).

9 *I am writing my reveries entirely for myself*: on the relationship between Rousseau's *Reveries* and Montaigne's *Essays*, see the Introduction, above, pp. xix–xxiii.

12 *the rue du Chemin vert*: this road, which still exists today, led from what was then the Rue de la Contrescarpe (now the Boulevard Beaumarchais) north-eastwards to the heights where the Père Lachaise Cemetery is now situated and onwards past the hamlet of Ménilmontant to the village of Charonne. Both the hamlet and the village were only absorbed into the city of Paris in 1860.

the picris hieracioides of the Compositae family: commonly known as hawk-weed ox-tongue.

the bupleurum falcatum of the Umbelliferae family: commonly known as hare's ear root.

the cerastium aquaticum: of the Caryophyllaceae family and commonly known as water chickweed.

I placed in my collection: on Rousseau's interest in botany, see the Introduction, above, pp. xvi–xvii.

13 *the Galant Jardinier*: a cabaret in Paris.

14 *a carriage*: belonging to Michel Étienne Le Peletier de Saint-Fargeau (1736–78), the president of the Parlement de Paris.

15 *'At the Haute Borne'*: literally 'The Upper Milepost', a reference to the upper part of the rue de Ménilmontant (the present-day rue Oberkampf), beyond the intersection of the rue du Bas Pincourt (the present-day rue Saint-Maur).

the Temple: a reference to the Enclosure of the Temple where the Priory of the Knights Templar and the Tower of the Temple were located; both were demolished in 1811, and today only the Square du Temple remains.

the half-league: approximately two kilometres.

rue Plâtrière: the present-day rue Jean-Jacques Rousseau.

My wife's cries: Rousseau married Thérèse Levasseur (1721–1801) in 1768, though they had been together since 1745.

16 *I have always hated shadows*: see also Book 11 of the *Confessions*: 'My nat-ural tendency is to fear shadows; I dread and detest their air of darkness; mystery always disturbs me; it is too antipathetic to my own nature, which is open to the point of imprudence' (p. 553).

Monsieur Lenoir, the police lieutenant general: Jean-Charles-Pierre Lenoir (1732–1807) was lieutenant general of police in Paris from 1774 to 1785.

Madame d'Ormoy: Charlotte Chaumet d'Ormoy (1732?–91) was the author of a one-act *opéra-comique* performed at Versailles, entitled *Zelmis, or the*

Young Savage (*Zelmis, ou la jeune sauvage*, 1780), a short story entitled *The Lama in Love* (*Le Lama amoureux*, 1781), and two novels: *The Misfortunes of Young Emélie* (*Les Malheurs de la jeune Emélie*, 1777), to which Rousseau refers here, and *Wavering Virtue, or the Life of Mlle d'Amincourt* (*La Vertu chancelante, ou la vie de Mlle d'Amincourt*, 1778), which she dedicated to Frederick of Prussia, though her authorship is disputed.

the Queen: Marie Antoinette (1755–93) had been queen since 1774.

what I thought of women writers: in Book 5 of *Émile*, Rousseau argues that women should attach more importance to their domestic duties than to any literary talents they may have: 'Even if a woman had real talent, any pretension on her part would diminish it. Her dignity lies in being unknown, her glory lies in her husband's esteem, and her pleasures lie in her family's happiness.'

17 *all printed and even bound*: an allusion to the conventional practice at the time of selling books unbound in the first instance; having it bound was a sign of the value that Mme d'Ormoy attached to her gift.

I found it quite unpleasant: the Introduction to Mme d'Ormoy's *The Misfortunes of Young Emélie* includes exaggerated praise of Rousseau as being nothing short of her hero: 'I know of nobody with a more sensitive soul. . . . I confess that this famous man is my hero, but since to praise his virtues is above a vulgar pen, and since a woman's pen in particular is too weak to paint his portrait, I shall say nothing and be content to admire him, paying him in the depths of my heart the homage he deserves.'

her daughter: Anne-Jeanne-Félicité d'Ormoy (1765–1830), who would go on to marry the writer Simon-Pierre Mérard de Saint-Just and publish a number of works of her own, including a poem entitled *The Four Ages of Man* (*Les quatre âges de l'homme*, 1782) and a Gothic novel entitled *The Dark Castle, or The Sufferings of Young Ophelle* (*Le Château noir ou les souffrances de la jeune Ophelle*, 1798).

a footnote: at the end of Part I of *The Misfortunes of Young Emélie*, Mme d'Ormoy inserted an addendum, giving a passage to be inserted earlier in the novel, where there are three lines of dots. The text to be inserted includes stinging criticism of court society, and in particular monarchs who, since they listen only to what their courtiers tell them, neglect their people's welfare: 'If sovereigns knew all the wrong that is done in their name, they would weep at being kings. The whole purpose of royalty is to ensure people's happiness, and this is the duty of a virtuous king, but it is difficult to make the truth reach as far as the throne; indeed, great care is taken to keep well away anyone who might tell the truth: the king's people are dying of hunger, but they are presented to him as being happy.'

18 *the Tuileries*: the gardens that extend west from the present-day Louvre in Paris.

the King: Louis XVI (1754–93) had been king since 1774.

18 *the Avignon Courier . . . funeral oration*: on 20 December 1776 the *Avignon Courier* (*Le Courrier d'Avignon*) included the following item, written by the paper's Paris correspondent on 12 December: 'M. Jean-Jacques Rousseau has died from the effects of his fall. He lived in poverty, he died wretchedly, and the strangeness of his fate accompanied him all the way to his grave. We are sorry not to be able to speak of the talents of this eloquent writer; our readers should be aware that the way he abused those talents forces us to say absolutely nothing here. There is every reason to believe that the public will not be deprived of his life story and that even the name of the dog that killed him will be found in it.' The newspaper subsequently corrected this false report on the following 31 December, in an item dated 21 December.

19 *if it had been God's will*: St Augustine seems not to have made this point, unless Rousseau is alluding to, and possibly misremembering, his argument that, even if there were no hope of divine salvation, it would still be preferable to strive for virtue and struggle against sin rather than simply give in to the latter (*The City of God*, XI. 15).

20 *Growing older, I continue learning*: a quotation from Plutarch's *Life of Solon*, 2. 2 and 31. 3. Solon (*c*.638–558 BC) was an Athenian statesman, lawmaker, and elegiac poet. Plutarch's *Lives* were translated into French by Jacques Amyot in 1559. In Book 1 of the *Confessions* Rousseau tells of the reading he did with his father at an early age, which included Plutarch's *Lives*: 'Plutarch, in particular, became my favourite author. The pleasure I took in reading and rereading him cured me in part of my passion for romances, and I soon preferred Agesilaus, Brutus, and Aristides to Orondate, Artamène, and Juba' (pp. 8–9); see also the Fourth Walk (p. 33).

in the last twenty years: since Rousseau appears to have written the Third Walk early in 1777, this is presumably a reference to his break with Mme d'Épinay and his departure from the Hermitage in December 1757. Rousseau evokes his stay on Mme d'Épinay's estate in the Ninth Walk (see p. 101).

22 *a minister full of wisdom and religion*: a reference to Jean-Jacques Lambercier (1676–1738), the pastor of the village of Bossey, near Geneva (now in the French *département* of Haute-Savoie), who educated Rousseau from the age of ten, together with his cousin Abraham, as Rousseau relates in Book 1 of the *Confessions* (pp. 12–24).

Madame de Warens: Rousseau, then aged fifteen, met Françoise-Louise de la Tour, the baronne de Warens (1699–1762), in Annecy, where she had fled to escape an unhappy marriage, in March 1728. Paid to seek out and assist potential converts to Catholicism, she sent Rousseau to Turin for instruction, and on 21 April 1728 he abjured Protestantism before being baptized a Catholic two days later. Rousseau and Mme de Warens subsequently became lovers, as Rousseau recalls in the Tenth Walk (p. 107). See also Book 2 of the *Confessions* (pp. 47–9, 53–4).

Fénelon: François de Salignac de la Mothe-Fénelon (1651–1715), arch-bishop of Cambrai, to whom Rousseau also alludes in Book 6 of the *Confessions* (p. 223).

23 *my fortune seemed to be about to become more firmly established*: Rousseau turned forty in June 1752, by which time he had written and published articles on music for Diderot and d'Alembert's *Encyclopedia* (*L'Encyclopédie*, 1751–72) and had won the Dijon Academy essay prize with what was to become his *Discourse on the Sciences and the Arts* (*Discours sur les sciences et les arts*, 1751); in October 1752 his opera *The Village Soothsayer* (*Le Devin du village*) would be performed to great acclaim before the King at Fontainebleau.

a good, solid woollen coat: see also Rousseau's account in Book 8 of the *Confessions*: 'I began my reform with that of my appearance; I gave up gold trimmings and white stockings, took to a short wig, laid aside my sword, and sold my watch, saying to myself as I did so, with a feeling of unbeliev-able joy: *I will never again, thank God, need to know what time it is*' (p. 354).

24 *a position for which I was in no way suited*: a reference to Rousseau's appoint-ment in July 1752 as cashier in the office of Charles-Louis Dupin de Francueil (1716–80), receiver general, a post from which he resigned later that year.

a different moral world that was opening up before me: a possible allusion to the 'illumination' he experienced on his way to visit Diderot in prison at Vincennes in August 1749, when he read about the prize-essay topic set by the Dijon Academy on whether or not the progress of the sciences and arts had purified morals. Rousseau describes this experience in Book 8 of his *Confessions* (pp. 341–2).

modern philosophers: an allusion primarily to Diderot, Grimm, d'Alembert, and d'Holbach.

27 *Profession of Faith of the Savoyard Vicar*: the *Profession of Faith of the Savoyard Vicar* (*Profession de foi du vicaire savoyard*) was inserted in Book 4 of *Émile*. It is an account of the nature and basis of religious belief, in the course of which Rousseau criticizes the importance often attached in religion to miracles and revelation; he also criticizes the intolerance that exists between different religious denominations. It was primarily because of this *Profession* that *Émile* was condemned by the Roman Catholic authorities.

33 *How to Profit by One's Enemies*: in this essay (*De capienda ex inimicis util-itate*) in his *Moralia*, which Jacques Amyot had translated into French in 1572, Plutarch argues that not only need one not suffer harm from one's enemies, but one can in fact gain from them. For example, our enemies force us to be watchful for ourselves and not make the same mistakes that we condemn in them; it is also possible to demonstrate a number of virtues better in relationships with enemies than with friends, such as gentleness, forbearance, and magnanimity.

33 *a volume of the abbé Rozier's journal*: the abbé François Rozier (1734–93), a
    Jesuit priest and keen botanist, was the founding editor of the *Journal of
    Physics and Natural History* (*Journal de physique et d'histoire naturelle*),
    first published in 1771. Rousseau had met Rozier in Lyon in 1768 and had
    enjoyed his company, but by 1777 Rousseau evidently saw him as another
    of his enemies. The specific reference here may be to the August 1776
    issue of the *Journal*, in which Rozier announced the foundation in Geneva
    of a society for the arts.

    Vitam vero impendenti, Rozier: the Latin phrase, meaning 'to the one who
    consecrates his life to truth', is a modified quotation from Juvenal, 'vitam
    impendero vero' (*Satires*, IV. 91), meaning 'to consecrate one's life to
    truth', which Rousseau had first used as his personal motto in 1758 in the
    Letter to d'Alembert on Theatre (*Lettre à d'Alembert sur les spectacles*).

    the Know thyself of the Temple at Delphi: this Ancient Greek aphorism was
    inscribed in the forecourt of the Temple of Apollo at Delphi. Rousseau
    also refers to it at the beginning of the preface to the *Discourse on Inequality*
    (*Discours sur l'origine et les fondements de l'inégalité*, 1755): 'Of all the areas
    of human knowledge, the most valuable but least advanced seems to be that
    of man, and I venture that the inscription on the temple at Delphi, for all
    its brevity, expresses a precept of greater importance and difficulty than all
    the thick tomes of moralists' (trans. Franklin Philip, ed. Patrick Coleman
    (Oxford: Oxford University Press, 1994), 14).

    an awful lie: a reference to the episode in Turin in 1728, when Rousseau,
    following the death of his employer Mme de Vercellis, stole a ribbon
    but blamed the theft on Marion, a servant girl who also worked in the
    household. Rousseau recounts this episode in Book 2 of the *Confessions*
    (pp. 82–3).

34 *a truth that one should make known*: it is unclear which book Rousseau is
    referring to, though it could be Samuel von Pufendorf's *On the Law of
    Nature and of Nations* (*De jure naturae et gentium*, 1672) or Claude Adrien
    Helvétius's *On the Mind* (*De l'Esprit*, 1758), both of which discuss lying
    and both of which Rousseau knew well.

38 *The Temple of Cnidus*: a reference to *Le Temple de Gnide*, a pastoral allegory
    about nymphs and shepherds in love, written by Montesquieu, who first
    published it anonymously in 1725 with a preface, supposedly written by
    the translator of a work found in the library of a Greek bishop. Cnidus
    (modern-day Tekir in Turkey) was an ancient Greek city of Caria where
    there was a temple of Aphrodite.

42 *in order to have something to say*: see also Book 3 of the *Confessions*, in which
    Rousseau bemoans his 'slowness of thought': his ideas, he says, are 'con-
    fused, slow to take shape, and only ever occur to me afterwards' (p. 110).

43 *Monsieur Foulquier*: a reference to François-Joseph Foulquier (1744–89), a
    naturalist and engraver who went on to become the Intendant first of
    Guadeloupe and then of Martinique, where he died.

Benoît: a reference to Pierre-Antoine Benoît (1721?–96?), future editor, with the marquis de Girardin, of a posthumous collection of Rousseau's musical works, entitled *Consolations for the Miseries of My Life* (*Consolations des misères de ma vie*, 1781).

I had not had that happiness: this is untrue, since between 1746 and 1752, Rousseau and Thérèse had had five children, all of whom they gave up to the Foundlings' Hospital.

45 *to lay claim to virtue*: this paragraph recalls the opening of Book 1 of the *Confessions*: 'I have concealed nothing that was ill, added nothing that was good, and if I have sometimes used some indifferent ornamentation, this has only ever been to fill a void occasioned by my lack of memory; I may have supposed to be true what I knew could have been so, never what I knew to be false' (p. 5).

painting myself in profile: this is the very criticism Rousseau levels at Montaigne in the preface to his *Confessions* in the Neuchâtel manuscript of that work: 'Montaigne offers us a likeness, but in profile' (p. 644).

had a calico works there: in 1706, having learned how to manufacture printed cotton in Holland, Antoine Fazy (1681–1731) opened his own factory in Les Pâquis, north of Geneva. In 1719 he married his third wife, Clermonde Rousseau (1674–1747), Rousseau's aunt.

46 *Magnanima menzogna! . . . Si bello che si possa a te preporre?*: 'Oh noble lie! Did ever truth presume | to claim with fairer title virtue's throne?' (Tasso, *The Liberation of Jerusalem* (1580–1), II. 22, trans. Max Wickert, ed. Mark Davie (Oxford: Oxford University Press, 2009), 26). In Tasso's epic poem, Sophronia, a Christian maiden of Jerusalem, confesses to a crime she has not committed in order to save the Christians from being massacred by the Muslim king. Rousseau was an avid reader of Tasso, to whose works he may have been introduced by the abbé de Gouvon as early as 1728, as he mentions in Book 3 of the *Confessions* (p. 95); in 1771–2 he began a prose translation of the story of Sophronia, which was first published posthumously in 1781, though it does not include the couplet quoted here.

a game of mall: an early modern French mallet-and-ball game, a precursor of croquet.

Plain-Palais: an area of open land to the south-west of Geneva.

47 *I have not committed it*: see also Book 1 of the *Confessions*, in which Rousseau admits that 'it is not what is criminal that is the hardest to reveal, but what is laughable or shameful' (p. 17).

49 *the Lac de Bienne*: a lake in the west of Switzerland. Rousseau stayed on the Île de St Pierre for six weeks from 12 September to 25 October 1765, a stay he also describes in Book 12 of the *Confessions* (pp. 623–34).

half a league: see the note to p. 15, above.

50 *the stoning at Môtiers*: a reference to the stones thrown by a mob at Rousseau's house in Môtiers, a village in the Val-de-Travers in Neuchâtel, during the night of 6 September 1765.

50 *the first signs of which I was already beginning to detect*: a reference to the role of David Hume and the comtesse de Boufflers in persuading Rousseau to travel to England in 1766.

two months on this island: Rousseau was ordered to leave the island by the senators of Bern on 16 October 1765.

51 *far niente*: an Italian phrase meaning 'do nothing'.

a man dedicated to idleness: see also Rousseau's evocation of idleness in Book 12 of the *Confessions*: 'The idleness I like is not that of the lounger, who sits there, arms crossed, wholly inert, and who no more thinks than he acts. It is at once that of the child, who is always in motion and always doing nothing, and that of the driveller, who rambles on endlessly while never stirring from his seat' (p. 627).

Doctor d'Ivernois: Jean-Antoine d'Ivernois (1703–65), a doctor and naturalist from Môtiers. Rousseau notes in Book 12 of the *Confessions* that 'the taste for botany I had begun to acquire from Doctor d'Ivernois, lending new interest to my walks, led me to ramble round the whole region, herborizing' (p. 617).

Flora petrinsularis: that is, a work about the flora of the Île de St Pierre.

52 *Systema naturae*: the *System of Nature* (1735) is one of the major works of the Swedish botanist, zoologist, and physician Carl Linnaeus (1707–78), in which he outlines his ideas for the hierarchical classification of the natural world, dividing it into the animal kingdom, the plant kingdom, and the mineral kingdom; the classification of the plant kingdom followed Linnaeus's new sexual system, with species with the same number of stamens being treated in the same group. In Book 12 of the *Confessions* Rousseau describes his 'passion' for Linnaeus's work, 'a passion of which I have never quite been able to cure myself, even after sensing its deficiencies' (p. 629).

La Fontaine asked if they had read Habakkuk: Rousseau seemingly misremembers here an anecdote told by Louis Racine in his *Memoir on the Life of Jean Racine* (*Mémoire sur la vie de Jean Racine*, 1752) about his father and La Fontaine, when Racine had given the fabulist a bible to flick through during a church service: 'La Fontaine chanced upon the prayer of the Jews in Baruch, and overcome with admiration, he said to my father: "This Baruch was a great genius: who was he?" The next day and for several days thereafter, whenever he met someone he knew in the street, he would, once the usual compliments had been paid, raise his voice and say: "Have you read Baruch? He was a great genius."' Instead of the Book of Baruch, one of the deuterocanonical books of the Bible (which are considered non-canonical by Protestants), Rousseau refers to the Book of Habakkuk, the eighth book of the twelve minor prophets of the Hebrew Bible.

53 *the pleasures of life*: see also Rousseau's account in Book 12 of the *Confessions*: 'Often, abandoning my boat to the mercy of wind and water, I would give

myself up to a reverie without object, and which, for being foolish, was none the less sweet' (p. 630).

the pilot of the Argonauts: an allusion to the Greek mythological hero Jason, who led the Argonauts in the quest for the Golden Fleece.

54 *took me by surprise*: see also Book 12 of the *Confessions*: 'I have always loved water passionately; the sight of it plunges me into a delicious reverie, which often, however, has no determinate object' (p. 628).

the excessively complicated modern ones: this recalls Rousseau's *Letter on French Music* (*Lettre sur la musique française*, 1753), in which he criticizes modern French music as being marred by complicated harmony and counterpoint. The *Letter* was one of Rousseau's interventions in the so-called 'Quarrel of the Buffoons' in the early 1750s, which opposed proponents of French and Italian music, and which Rousseau discusses in Book 8 of the *Confessions* (pp. 374–6).

fifteen years later: in fact only twelve years later, since Rousseau left the Île de St Pierre in 1765 and wrote the Fifth Walk in all likelihood in spring 1777.

59 *the new boulevard*: a reference to the present-day boulevard Raspail.

the Bièvre: a river that flows up from the south of Paris and into the Seine close to the Île de la Cité, though today it is buried in tunnels for its whole course within the city.

Gentilly: a village south of Paris; it was annexed to become part of the city in 1860.

the Barrière d'Enfer: this gate (literally the 'Barrier of Hell') was situated just north of what is today the Place Denfert-Rochereau in the Montparnasse district in the south of Paris; it became, in 1784–91, part of the city wall built by the corporation of tax farmers, the Fermiers-Généraux, to ensure the payment to them of a tax on any goods entering Paris.

tisane: an infusion, often made in the eighteenth century with barley, liquorice, or couch-grass root and used for medicinal purposes.

61 *fulfil the duties of their position*: an echo, not of *Émile*, but of Book 5 of the *Confessions*: 'It is said that at dawn in Muslim countries a man goes about the streets ordering husbands to do their duty by their wives. I would be a bad Turk at such moments' (p. 186).

64 *was never betrayed*: a possible allusion to the attempt made in 1754 by Jean-Vincent Caperonnier de Gauffecourt (1691–1766), Rousseau's friend and fellow Genevan, to seduce his companion, Thérèse, by offering her money and showing her pornographic images, as Rousseau recounts in Book 8 of the *Confessions* (pp. 380–1).

66 *the ring of Gyges*: according to Plato's *Republic* (359d–360c), the shepherd Gyges, who was king of Lydia from 716 to 678 BC, had managed to murder his predecessor King Candaules and seduce his Queen thanks to a magic

ring he discovered that made him invisible. Plato uses the story of the ring of Gyges as a metaphor for the corruption caused by power: Glaucon recounts the story to Socrates, arguing that men are inherently unjust and are only restrained from unjust behaviour by the fetters of law and society.

67 *the Golden Legend*: a reference to the hagiographical work by Jacobus de Voragine (*c.*1230–98), the *Legenda aurea* (1261–6), which gives an account of 180 saints' lives and their miracles; it was one of the most popular religious works in medieval Europe.

St Medard: a reference to the tomb of François de Pâris (1690–1727), a well-known Jansenist deacon, in the cemetery of the church of St Médard in Paris, which quickly became a site of religious pilgrimage, with many pilgrims declaring that they had been miraculously cured, notably in 1731 and 1732, when a large number of cases of convulsions, particularly amongst women, were recorded.

68 *I am incapable of doing good*: see also Book 3 of the *Confessions*: 'I would enjoy society as much as the next man, if I were not certain to show myself there not only to my own disadvantage, but as quite different from what I am' (p. 114).

rarely of commission: in Christian theology, a sin of commission is a positive act contrary to some prohibitive precept, whereas a sin of omission is a failure to do what is commanded. See also Book 10 of the *Confessions*: 'My worst faults have been those of omission: I have rarely done what I ought not to have done, and unfortunately I have even more rarely done what I ought' (p. 497).

69 *Murray's Regnum vegetabile*: the Swedish botanist Johan Andreas Murray (1740–91), a disciple of Linnaeus, published in 1774 the thirteenth edition of the *System of Nature* (see the note to p. 52, above) under the title *System of the Vegetable Kingdom* (*Systema vegetabilium*), which included his own introduction, entitled *The Vegetable Kingdom* (*Regnum vegetabile*).

70 *a painful and unappealing occupation*: see also Part I of the *Discourse on Inequality*: 'If nature has destined us to be healthy, I would almost venture to assert that the state of reflection is contrary to nature and that the man who meditates is a perverse animal' (p. 30).

71 *by outside forces*: a reference to the publication of the *Discourse on the Sciences and the Arts* in 1751.

72 *drugs and medicine*: see also Book 5 of the *Confessions*: 'I know of no other study that is more compatible with my own natural bent than that of plants, and indeed the life I have led in the country these past ten years has been more or less one continual herborization, although without, it is true, either objective or progress; but having at the time no notion of what botany was, I viewed it with a sort of contempt and even disgust, as being of interest only to apothecaries. . . . Thus it was that botany, chemistry, and anatomy, all of which were confused in my mind under the general title of

medicine, served only to supply me with an endless succession of sarcastic jokes and to earn me an occasional box on the ears' (p. 176).

Theophrastus: a student of Aristotle and Plato, Theophrastus (*c*.371–*c*.287 BC) wrote, amongst other things, two major botanical works, *Enquiry into Plants* (*De historia plantarum*) and *On the Causes of Plants* (*De causis plantarum*), which were the first systematic study of the botanical world and which greatly influenced medieval science.

Dioscorides: the Greek physician, pharmacologist, and botanist Pedanius Dioscorides (*c*.40–*c*.90) is best known as the author of the five-book work *On Medical Matters* (*De materia medica*), detailing the herbs and remedies used by the Greeks, Romans, and other cultures of antiquity.

77 *anatomy*: see also Book 6 of the *Confessions*: 'What set the seal on my dis-quiet was that I had included some physiology in my reading and had begun to study anatomy, so that, constantly revising the multitude and functioning of the parts of which my system was composed, I expected to feel it going wrong twenty times a day; far from being surprised at finding myself dying, I was amazed that I should still be alive; I had only to read the description of an illness to be quite certain that I was suffering from it' (p. 242).

79 *La Robella*: situated on the north face of the Chasseron mountain, above the village of Buttes, in the Jura, Switzerland.

Clerc: Jean-Henri Clerc was a surgeon and judge in the civil court in Val-de-Travers; he was also a confidant of Rousseau's long-standing friend Mme Boy de la Tour.

80 *nidus avis*: bird's-nest orchid.

the large laserpitium: presumably the *laserpitium latifolium*, or laserwort.

lycopodium: a genus of clubmosses, also known as ground pines or creeping cedar.

Montmollin: Frédéric Guillaume de Montmollin (1709–83), Protestant minister of Môtiers. Originally a friend of Rousseau, Montmollin turned against him after the scandal surrounding the *Letters Written from the Mountain* (*Lettres écrites de la montagne*, 1764), in which Rousseau defended himself against the attacks made on him after the publication of *Émile* by the Genevan authorities, whose abuses of authority he also set about exposing; these *Letters* were in turn condemned, under pressure from Geneva, by the authorities in Neuchâtel, and Montmollin subsequently fell into line. The term used by Rousseau to describe Montmollin here, 'prédicant', which literally means 'preacher', was in the eighteenth cen-tury a pejorative term for a Protestant minister.

the rue St Antoine: a long, wide road in Paris in Rousseau's time, running from the Bastille past the Place Royale (the present-day Place des Vosges) to the church of St Paul.

81 *Du Peyrou*: Pierre-Alexandre Du Peyrou (1729–94), a businessman from Neuchâtel who went on, as one of Rousseau's executors, to publish a

posthumous edition of his collected works; Rousseau refers to him in
Books 6 and 12 of the *Confessions* (pp. 221, 589).

81 *d'Escherny*: François-Louis d'Escherny (1733–1815), a writer whose works
include *The Lacunae of Philosophy* (*Les Lacunes de la philosophie*, 1783). He
went on to write a eulogy of Rousseau in 1789–90, which he published as
an introduction to his work *On Equality* (*De l'Égalité*, 1796); his memoirs,
published in 1811, include an admiring account of Rousseau, whom he
had first met in Paris in 1762.

Pury: Abram Pury (1724–1807), a former officer in the army in Sardinia,
who defended Rousseau against Montmollin; one of his daughters
married Du Peyrou in 1769. Rousseau refers to him in Book 12 of the
Confessions (p. 589).

Grenoble: Rousseau stayed in Grenoble from 11 July to 12 August 1768.

Bovier: Gaspard Bovier (1733?–1806), a lawyer in the Grenoble *parlement*;
he went on to write an account of Rousseau's stay in the town, first
published in 1898.

Isère: the Isère river, in south-eastern France, flows through Grenoble.

Dauphiné humility: the Dauphiné is a former province in south-eastern
France, the capital of which was Grenoble; in 1790 it was divided into
three *départements*: the current Isère, Drôme, and Hautes-Alpes.

hippophae: buckthorn.

86 *snuff out my lantern*: an allusion to Diogenes of Sinope (412?–323 BC), who
walked through Athens carrying a lantern in daylight, looking for an honest
man. See also Part II of the *Discourse on Inequality*: '[The attentive reader]
will understand that because the human race of one era is not the human
race of another, Diogenes could not find a man because he searched among
his contemporaries for a man from a time that no longer was' (p. 83).

88 *yoke of public opinion*: Rousseau's distinction here between self-love
(*amour-propre*) and love of self (*amour de soi*) recalls his *Discourse on
Inequality*, in which he argues that society's negative influence on humankind is seen in particular in its transformation of love of self into self-love,
or vanity (p. 115).

89 *anxious and unhappy*: see also Book 3 of the *Confessions*: 'For me, foresight
has always been the ruin of enjoyment. Seeing into the future has availed
me nothing; I have never been able to avoid it' (pp. 103–4).

93 *one of my reveries*: see the Fifth Walk, above.

94 *Monsieur P.*: presumably a reference to Pierre Prévost (1751–1839), a
Genevan and tutor to the children of Etienne Delessert who went on to
translate Euripides and Adam Smith; he visited Rousseau in the last two
years of his life.

Madame Geoffrin: Marie-Thérèse Geoffrin (1699–1777) was one of the
leading women in the French Enlightenment, hosting an important salon
in Paris attended by major writers and freethinkers. Following her death

on 6 October 1777, d'Alembert published his eulogy of her, the *Letter from M. d'Al*** to M. the Marquis de C*** [Condorcet] about Madame Geoffrin* (*Lettre de M. d'Al*** à M. le Marquis de C*** sur Madame Geoffrin*), in which he observes: 'Madame Geoffrin had all the tastes of a sensitive and sweet soul: she loved children passionately; she could not see a single one without being moved; she was drawn by the innocence and the weakness of their youth. . . . She enjoyed talking with them and asking them questions, and she could not abide their governesses prompting their answers. "I prefer", she used to say to them, "to hear his own inanities rather than those you dictate to him. . . . I wish one question could be asked of all those unfortunate people who are going to be put to death for their crimes: Did you love children? I am sure their answer will be no".'

95 *Military Academy*: the Royal Military Academy (L'École royale militaire) in Paris was founded by Louis XV in 1751, with the help of Madame de Pompadour and the financier Pâris-Duverney, in order to offer a military training to men from humble backgrounds.

Foundlings' Hospital: following on from the work done amongst the poor by the Catholic priest Vincent de Paul (1581–1660), the Paris Foundlings' Hospital (L'Hôpital des Enfants-Trouvés) was founded by Louis XIV in 1670. To begin with, abandoned children were gathered into several existing houses scattered around the city, until 1748, when it was decided to erect a dedicated building close to the cathedral of Notre-Dame. From the time of its founding, the number of children brought to the Foundlings' Hospital each year grew rapidly: in 1670, 312 children were admitted; in 1680, 890; in 1700, 1,738; in 1740, 3,150; and by the end of the eighteenth century, more than 6,000 children were being admitted each year. It was Voltaire who, in his pamphlet *The Feeling of the Citizens* (*Le Sentiment des citoyens*, 1764), revealed that Rousseau had abandoned his children to the Foundlings' Hospital; convinced that he was now under attack from both religious authorities and intellectuals, Rousseau responded by starting to write his *Confessions*.

96 *a thousand times worse*: see also Book 8 of the *Confessions*: 'In handing over my children to be raised at public expense, since I had not the means to bring them up myself, in ensuring that they became labourers and peasants rather than adventurers and fortune-seekers, I believed that I was acting as a true citizen and father, and I looked upon myself as a member of Plato's republic. On more than one occasion since, my heartfelt regrets have told me that I was mistaken, but far from my reason offering me the same advice, I have often thanked heaven for having preserved them from their father's destiny, and from the one that threatened to be their lot if I had been forced to abandon them' (pp. 347–8).

What Mahomet did to Séide: in Voltaire's tragedy *Mahomet* (1742), Mahomet persuades Séide to kill his father.

98 *Nouvelle France*: a district (literally 'New France') to the north of Paris, and just east of the hill of Montmartre, along and around the rue

Sainte-Anne (the present-day rue du Faubourg-Poissonnière), so called because it was the site of a barracks, built in 1772 to house recruits, often press-ganged from local cabarets, who were to go and serve in Canada.

98 *Clignancourt*: a village to the north of Paris, it was annexed to the city in 1860.

Nanterre cakes: the town of Nanterre, to the west of Paris, was famous in the eighteenth century for its salt pork and cakes.

99 *écu*: a silver coin worth six *livres*. In 1764 the statesman and economist Jacques Turgot drew up a table of upper levels of wealth, in which he indicated that an annual income of 6,000 *livres* was decent, but by no means rich; in the provinces, 12,000 *livres* was the minimum income with which one could be considered rich, in Paris, 15,000. At the other end of the spectrum, a manual labourer could expect to earn 1 *livre* a day.

Porte Maillot: one of the gates into the Bois de Boulogne to the west of Paris, which was a royal park when Rousseau was writing.

La Muette: a reference to the royal château on the edge of the Bois de Boulogne, near the Porte de la Muette; it was demolished in 1793.

Passy: a village to the west of Paris near the Bois de Boulogne; it was annexed to the city in 1860.

looking for customers: cone-shaped wafers—or *oublies* in French, from *oblata*, the Latin word for the consecrated host—could be had in a kind of lottery by buying chances from a seller (often former soldiers, hence the drum) equipped with a numbered wheel, on which there was a spinning arrow; a customer would buy a spin and receive the number of wafers indicated by the section on which the arrow stopped, though it was known that sellers could determine where the arrow would stop by means of a hidden magnet. There is a painting of a wafer-seller plying his wares by Louis Watteau, painted in 1785 and now in the Musée des Beaux-Arts in Lille, France.

liards: a copper coin worth just 3 *deniers*, or a quarter of a *sol*, which was worth 12 *deniers*; 1 *livre* (see note above) was worth 20 *sols* or the equivalent of 80 *liards*.

100 *sols*: see note to p. 99, above.

louis: a gold coin worth 24 *livres*.

101 *La Chevrette*: the château belonging to Denis-Joseph Lalive d'Épinay (1724–82) and his well-connected wife Louise d'Épinay (1726–83) in the Montmorency valley, north of Paris. In April 1756 Madame d'Épinay lent Rousseau a cottage in the grounds of La Chevrette, known as The Hermitage, for which he left Paris and where he stayed until the end of 1757, working, amongst other things, on *Julie*. The celebrations Rousseau refers to here are those held for Monsieur d'Épinay on 9 October 1757: see Book 9 of the *Confessions* (p. 454).

the dragon guarding it: in Greek mythology, the Hesperides are nymphs who, aided by a hundred-headed dragon called Ladon, tend and guard the blissful garden of Hera, wife of Zeus, where immortality-giving golden apples grow; the eleventh labour of Hercules was to steal the apples.

102 *enjoying the day's pleasures*: this echoes Rousseau's *Letter to d'Alembert*, in which he praises popular festivities and condemns the artificial pleasures of Parisian theatres.

103 *their masters' hospitality*: see also Book 10 of the *Confessions*: 'Although I restricted my humble largesse to houses where I was a frequent visitor, it none the less proved ruinous. . . . These expenses are unavoidable for a man of my temperament, who is incapable of acquiring anything or of improvising anything for himself, and who cannot bear the presence of a valet who grumbles and who serves you grudgingly' (pp. 503–4).

104 *Invalides*: a hospital in Paris for injured soldiers, founded by Louis XIV in 1670.

We were . . . Young, valiant, and brave: a quotation from Plutarch's *Life of Lycurgus*, 21. 3—the legendary lawgiver of Sparta—in the French translation by Amyot.

105 *Île des Cygnes*: a small island ('Swan Island') in the Seine in Paris, near the Invalides.

107 *Palm Sunday*: the date in question is 12 April 1778.

Madame de Warens: Rousseau first met Mme de Warens on 21 March 1728; see the note to p. 22, above.

born with the century: Mme de Warens was born on 31 March 1699.

not yet seventeen: Rousseau, who was born on 28 June 1712, was in fact fifteen when he first met Mme de Warens.

the rest of my days: see also Book 2 of the *Confessions*: 'I saw Mme de Warens. This was the period of my life that decided my character' (p. 47).

sent me away: a reference to Rousseau's trip to Turin, where he became a Roman Catholic.

for seven of them: the Roman historian Cassius Dio (*Roman History*, LXIX. 19. 2) attributes this remark to Servius Sulpicius Similis, commander of the Emperor's bodyguards from 112 to 119 during the reigns of Trajan and Hadrian, not Vespasian. Moreover, Similis was not disgraced, but simply resigned from his role, which he had taken up reluctantly; he had the remark about his life inscribed on his tombstone.

108 *Mama*: Rousseau's affectionate name for Mme de Warens.

our refuge: a reference to Les Charmettes, near Chambéry, where Rousseau and Mme de Warens lived in 1735–6.